THE SOUTH DOWNS WAY
&
THE DOWNS LINK

SOUTH DOWNS WAY
    Eastbourne - Winchester ... 102 miles
    (East Sussex, West Sussex, Hampshire)

DOWNS LINK
    St. Martha's - Botolphs ... 33 miles
    (Surrey, West Sussex)

THE SOUTH DOWNS WAY
&
THE DOWNS LINK

by
Kev Reynolds

CICERONE PRESS
MILNTHORPE, CUMBRIA

ISBN 1 85284 023 4

CONTENTS

Introduction 7
The Walks 9
The Southern Landscape 10
Accommodation 11
Walks for Everyone 12
Equipment for the Walks 14
Using the Guide 14

The South Downs Way 17
West Bound

Section 1:   Eastbourne to Alfriston (via The Seven Sisters) 21
Section 1a: Eastbourne to Alfriston (via Jevington) 27
Section 2:   Alfriston to Rodmell 34
Section 3:   Rodmell to Newmarket Inn 40
Section 4:   Newmarket Inn to Pyecombe 44
Section 5:   Pyecombe to Botolphs 50
Section 6:   Botolphs to Washington 54
Section 7:   Washington to Amberley Station 58
Section 8:   Amberley Station to Cocking 62
Section 9:   Cocking to South Harting 67
Section 10:   South Harting to Buriton 73
Section 11:   Buriton to Exton 75
Section 12:   Exton to Winchester 000

East Bound

Section 1:   Winchester to Exton 91
Section 2:   Exton to Buriton 94
Section 3:   Buriton to South Harting 96
Section 4:   South Harting to Cocking 96
Section 5:   Cocking to Amberley Station 98
Section 6:   Amberley Station to Washington 100

Section 7:   Washington to Botolphs 101
Section 8:   Botolphs to Pyecombe 102
Section 9:   Pyecombe to Newmarket Inn 104
Section 10:   Newmarket Inn to Rodmell 105
Section 11:   Rodmell to Alfriston 106
Section 12:   Alfriston to Eastbourne (via The Seven Sisters) 107
Section 12a: Alfriston to Eastbourne (via Jevington) 109

The Downs Link 111
South Bound
Section 1:   St. Martha's Hill to Cranleigh 115
Section 2:   Cranleigh to Rudgwick 119
Section 3:   Rudgwick to Christ's Hospital 123
Section 4:   Christ's Hospital to Partridge Green 126
Section 5:   Partridge Green to Botolphs 129

Useful Addresses 134
Recommended Further Reading 135

INTRODUCTION

The start to a bright spring day; striding through a gentle downland valley with the charming name of Cricketing Bottom, settling into that easy comfortable rhythm that is so essential to the full enjoyment of a long walk. The early sun warm overhead, my first cuckoo of the year calling from the hillside, the smoky haze of bluebells lining scrub-crowded slopes and the white froth of blackthorn creating haloes of flower. Only the pheasants complained. Larks rose singing, and all around swelled the Downs. Within an hour I'd be on their crest. Within an hour I'd be wandering alone save for the peewits and sky-larks and hares, save for the cowslips at my feet and the orchids in the spinneys. Alone with the lightest of breezes and with huge views that had the sea gleaming in one direction and the vast tartan plain of the low-lying Weald in the other. Hour upon hour wandering through history, past burial mounds left by the first wanderers of this Way, on land that once was covered by sea; serenaded day by day by minute specks of birds whose land this really is, on grasslands where slow-moving fluffs of sheep cropped hillsides that were darkened now and then by the sweeping shadows of clouds.

Cloud shadows; the only impatience on the South Downs Way.

* * *

Evening light, pure, soft and crystal clear after rain, shafted from the western hills where the beech crown of Chanctonbury Ring marked the silent beacon of the Downs. All drifted towards welcome twilight. A solitary blackbird warbled the Last Post. Ahead of me the track slid green and inviting between grassy banks for a quarter mile or more. Low fenced meadows on either side bore reeds and snaking water-courses where cattle grazed, but on the track itself dozens of rabbits had emerged to feed - safe, they'd assumed, from interruption. There were does and bucks and their young crouching, hopping, nibbling, cleansing. A scene, it was, transported from *Watership Down*, for this was Richard Adams' evening silflay. A peaceful scene. A timeless scene. A glimpse into nature's private world.

My walk was almost over for ahead, beyond the rabbits, were familiar shapes of the South Downs. Behind, and long lost from view, the lengthy blue swell of the North Downs. Between the two extremes

I'd had the multi-hued experience of the Downs Link that had taken some from each, but much more besides; another walk through the secret South.

*　*　*

The South is a surprisingly secret land, though its secrets are there to be unravelled if one only cares to look. It's a misjudged land, a misunderstood, often maligned land. Walking through it is the only way properly to discover its truths, for by wandering its ancient footpaths one absorbs its essence through the soles of the feet. Along the South Downs Way and the Downs Link one's field of vision is expanded with the miles to a greater knowledge of this secret land. The wanderer begins to appreciate that it is not so populous as is generally thought, that its countryside is infinitely more varied than might previously have been considered possible of 'the lowlands' and that when one comes onto the crest of the Downs, it is the very spaciousness of the scene that throws into disarray any preconceived ideas about the monopoly of mountains for landscape grandeur. The perspective fits. Scale is adjusted and beauty comes from order. In a world of constant change there is something very reassuring in a vast acreage of countryside that has somehow survived without too many scars. Another eye-opener for the rambler in the South.

There are other surprises too, but these must be left for the wanderer to discover for himself, for along the South Downs Way and the Downs Link there are journeys to be made that are full of delight. Journeys of discovery.

None but the walker can possibly understand the full extent of this statement, for it is only by the slowing of pace and total reliance upon yourself that one finds the ability to become part of the landscape. It is not something that can be achieved from the seat of a motor vehicle, for motor vehicles divorce you from the land. They take you through that land it is true, but at a pace too fast to be able to do anything but peer at a blurred vision, and that vision is made even more remote by a protection of metal and glass. Along country footpaths, however, you experience so much, from the succession of soil types beneath your feet to the *nuance* of every breeze that plays sculptor to the passing clouds. One breathes the fragrance of countless wayside plants, discovers the life of hedgerow and woodland shaw and drifts through an unfolding series of panoramas. If your senses are attuned to the world about you, the footpath becomes a highway of constant discovery, of constant delight.

Sheep on Downs above Kingston, near Lewes

The Walks

The South Downs Way leads for 102 miles between Eastbourne and Winchester, following the northern crest for much of the way and rarely descending to habitation except where river valleys interrupt the regular course of the hills. The Downs Link stretches 33 miles from St. Martha's Hill outside Guildford in Surrey to Botolph's not far from Steyning in Sussex. As its name suggests, this walk makes a link between the North Downs Way and the South Downs Way by striking in an almost direct line through the Weald.

They're very different walks. Each has its own particular quality. The South Downs Way, for example, gives broad panoramas; the Downs Link is largely tunnel vision. The South Downs Way is a long undulation, a switchback of hill and vale (Down and Bottom or Dean); the Downs Link is mostly on the level and die-straight mile after mile. The South Downs Way has been used in part since Neolithic times; the Downs Link owes its existence to Dr. Beeching's drastic re-shaping of Britain's railways in the early 1960s. Along the South Downs there are practically no watercourses except in a few cherished valleys; along the path of the Downs Link there are often rivers, streams, a section of canal and numerous little brooks for company. The South Downs Way is an officially approved long-distance footpath designated by the Countryside Commission; the

9

Downs Link is a recreation path devised jointly by Surrey and West Sussex County Councils and Waverley Borough Council. One will require almost a week to complete; the other needs only a couple of days.

Both will open your eyes to the multifarious pleasures of the English countryside and, hopefully, add something precious to your investment account of memory. They certainly have to mine.

The Southern Landscape

In the dark mists of time, from about 100 million to 70 million years ago, the land we now know as the Weald of south-east England lay beneath the waters of a warm, shallow sea, the bed of which was covered with sand and clay deposits. Miniscule shell-bearing organisms settled on this bed, the pure calcium carbonate of their shells powdering to a dust that built with staggering patience to a depth of just one foot every thirty thousand years or so. Consider the time-scale required to produce the chalk cliffs of Beachy Head - over 500 feet deep! Yet this layer of soft crumbling chalk, composed of all these tiny shells stretched from the Thames Valley to Pas de Calais and reached a depth of around 1,000 feet, and into this white cheese-like rock settled also the skeletons of sea sponges to form hard seams of flint.

Then came the great collision which built the Alps. Italy was thrust into Europe and Spain was pressured from the south. Mountains were slowly buckled and, as with a stone tossed into a pond, ripples spread in all directions. The chalk of southern England was forced into a huge dome that steadily emerged from the sea. Weathering followed; a process that continues to this day. Rain, wind, frost, each combined to nibble away at this vast dome, aided and abetted by rivers and streams that found a weakness when the chalk cracked as it buckled. The outer edges of the dome were last to crumble, the central core being carried away in the watercourses that flowed through it. The centre of that lost dome is now the Weald; the outer edges, the North and South Downs.

Rivers and streams still drain through the Weald, breaching the Downs in valleys far broader than they now require, while dry knuckle combes within the heart of the downland tell of streams that no longer exist.

When we ramble along the Downs today we may wonder at this triumph of history. Gazing from the clifftop at Beachy Head we see the body of the land exposed, carved through as though with a gigantic scalpel. We gaze into the heart of unfathomable time, at the crushed, bleached remnants of creatures whose sacrifice is our gain.

10

Later, as our route takes us away from the sea, that sacrifice is forgotten as we amble across grasslands rich with flowers. Yet beneath our boots the chalk lies deep and silent, waiting only for the plough to expose its weakness to the wind. Where the path leads through arable land we see polished flints littering the fields, the chalk cushion around them turning again to dust under the sun and wind, ready to be brushed away. Heights of the Downs shrinking in the summer breeze. One more act of sacrifice by the creatures that long ago gave their shells to our southern landscape.

We think of the Downs as a rolling flower-dazzled grassland cropped by sheep. Certainly they were largely so from the 14th century on and reaching a peak probably in the 19th century when the eastern portion of the Sussex Downs supported more than 200,000 ewes and lambs. But with the Second World War the whole nature of the South Downs began to change, and in the aftermath of hostilities vast acreages were turned by the plough for the production of grain. Today the wanderer of the Downs experiences a mixture of pasture, arable and woodland; a contrast that consists of meadows dancing with cowslips and the sharp golden dazzle of rape; of yellow-headed wheat in summer and the lush green foliage of beech and birch woods; of blackthorn scrub and harvest stubble.

In the Weald, that broad clay basin embraced by the arms of the Downs - North and South - there's a similar mixture of arable, pasture and woodland. But there are more woods and, nowadays, more pasture than arable. There are streams and hammer ponds that tell of the iron industy that first brought wealth to the Weald, and there are parkland estates spreading their acres of seclusion. On the Downs Link we experience a goodly assortment of landscapes that owe much to the centuries of care that have been lavished on them. There's a wide variety of trees and the radiance of light and shade, a chequerboard through which the track cuts a direct swathe.

On both walks we are shown some of the riches of this land. We tread paths of history, of colour and fragrance and grow to an awareness of the need to care for its frailty in the face of development and exploitation. For all the millenia of growth and weathering, this southern landscape has never been more vulnerable than it is today. Those who walk it learn to love it. Those who love it become determined to protect it for tomorrow.

Accommodation

Whilst it is feasible for both routes to be walked in dislocated day-sections with the aid of private (and in some cases, public) transport, this guide has been written mainly with the long-distance walker in mind, although the routes have been divided into modest stages for those who prefer to have intermediate collecting points. Accommodation details are therefore given at the end of each specific stage, where known. Addresses have been taken from English Tourist Board publications, but in some cases details change from year to year. The Ramblers' Association publishes a bed and breakfast guide listing recommended establishments situated near the routes of long-distance footpaths. This publication, available to members, is well worth studying. Advance booking is recommended (especially in the main summer months) in all cases, not only to ensure that room is available on the night required but, with regard to private bed and breakfast establishments, to check that accommodation is still on offer.

There are several Youth Hostels conveniently situated along the eastern section of the South Downs Way (plus one in Winchester at the end), and one about two miles from the finish of the Downs Link. Walkers planning to take advantage of hostel accommodation along the way are advised to arrange YHA membership prior to setting out on their walk, and to check well in advance the availability of beds on the nights required. The address of YHA National Office for membership details is given in the Appendix.

Unfortunately there is a marked shortage of campsites at present in the south of England, although determined backpackers may find sufficient farmers willing to allow an isolated overnight tent in a field. *Always* seek permission before settling a tent anywhere.

Walks for Everyone
Both these walks are gentle walks, ideal for family groups to tackle as well as for the more committed of long-distance striders. Both are well waymarked - not overly so, but sufficient for reassurance. Stiles and gates are among the best maintained of any I've ever used when walking in Britain. Paths underfoot are mostly firm and also well maintained, although the flint tracks of the western Downs may be a little uncomfortable for those not particularly well shod. There are a few muddy patches, naturally; more so in inclement weather. Downland chalk can be slippery after rain, Wealden clay can be boot-clinging and heavy.

The South Downs Way is bridle path throughout (there are one or two footpath-only stretches with bridle path alternatives), as is the Downs Link. There are few steep ascents or descents to face, but it should be borne in mind that for long periods on the South Downs Way the wanderer is fully exposed to the elements (wind, rain or sun)

Drinking water - for walkers and horses, on the South Downs Way

with no opportunity for shelter for several miles. Be suitably equipped.

If you're walking either of these routes end to end, you'll be surprised at the lack of villages or towns met along the way. This is one of the delights. There are occasional country pubs for refreshment, but remarkably few shops. Along the South Downs Way the Society of Sussex Downsmen, in conjunction with the Countryside Commission and local authorities, has been instrumental in arranging the provision of a number of drinking water taps for walkers and riders. But advice is given in any case to fill your drinking bottles at the start of each day's stage. Carry, too, food for the day. Rely too heavily on reaching a food store or a pub for refreshment and there's always the possibility that you'll arrive too late (or too early) to find it open!

Equipment for the Walks

No specialised equipment beyond one's normal walking gear will be necessary for tackling either route. Ramblers will be aware of the need for comfortable, well-fitting boots or stout shoes. Some may prefer to use 'trainers', but how these would stand up to some of the flint tracks of the Downs, I'm not sure. Certainly boots are preferable for the negotiation of muddy sections. Shorts will be comfortable wear on many stages at certain times of the year, although nettles or brambles tend in places to stray onto the pathway, and then leg protection will be needed. In our unsettled climate no walker will set out for five or six days or so without carrying waterproofs. Overtrousers are often handy for the crossing of hayfields or fields of corn after rain, or early in the morning with overnight dew still fresh.

A light rucksack should be adequate for the carrying of spare clothing, waterproofs and overnight toilet items. In addition a small first aid kit should be packed, plus food and drink for the day and any Ordnance Survey maps for an overview of the countryside through which the walk is leading.

Using the Guide

It is to be hoped that the clear waymarking with signposts experienced at practically all path junctions along both routes will mean that the sketch maps included within these pages will be sufficient to meet your mile-by-mile requirements. However, at the head of each section a note is given of the specific Ordnance Survey sheet covering the area described. The Landranger series 1:50,000 scale (1¼ inches = 1 mile) will provide an adequate overall picture of the route's progress. A grid reference is quoted here and there to enable you to locate your exact position with some ease.

Throughout the guide I have sought to give additional information on particularly interesting places and features seen along the way. In the text these are marked with a cross reference number, and information is outlined at the end of each section corresponding with this text number.

The routes, as written, are as they appeared when I walked them. It is inevitable that changes will occur. Who can predict hurricane-force winds that level woodlands? Who knows what the E E.C. will command of our farmers next? Who can tell what planning applications will meet with approval, thus building where today no building stands? It is my belief, though, that much of the countryside traversed by these two walks will vary only slightly with time. Both paths are well-established, waymarked and maintained. Any variation from the described routes, therefore, should be contained.

Notification of any major changes encountered along the way will be borne in mind for future editions of this book. A postcard detailing these, sent to me c/o the publisher, will be gratefully received.

In these days of competitive and record breaking walks there is a tendency for many to rush through the countryside with one eye on the hands of a watch and no time for contemplation of the intricacies of the landscape, no time for a leisurely absorption of nature's gifts - the pleasures that are there for all to enjoy. There is much more to walking a long distance path than burning the miles hour after hour. If you open your eyes, heart and mind to the splendours of the world about you, you'll grow richer by the day. So, as an antedote to the single-minded attitude of getting from A to B as quickly as possible, I have specifically written this guide with a more relaxed outlook in mind, and have attempted to bring out the flavour of these walks by including a few brief anecdotal snippets.

Nothing extraordinarily earth-shattering happened as I walked the South Downs Way or the Down Link. The southern counties do not lend themselves to major epics. But minute by minute I experienced the wonders of the countryside; *our* countryside, held in trust for the children of tomorrow. In that countryside was revealed the truly remarkable nature of the ordinary common scenes and pleasures that all may witness when out wandering the footpaths of our land. Noting these little snippets that add much to the eventual total of life's package of pleasures, it is my hope that the text will be enlivened and so inspire others who follow to absorb as much of the landscape and the creatures that people it, as possible.

It is a lovely world and life is a gift; please don't take either for granted.

* * *

While walking these routes it is my fervent hope that you gain much enjoyment from the countryside. But remember that it needs your care and respect.

* Guard against all risk of fire
* Fasten all gates
* Keep dogs under close control
* Keep to public paths across farmland
* Use gates and stiles to cross fences, hedges and walls
* Leave livestock, crops and machinery alone
* Take your litter home
* Help to keep all water clean
* Protect wildlife, plants and trees
* Take special care on country roads
* Make no unnecessary noise

The Country Code quoted above follows in the wake of principles set by Octavia Hill, a champion of the countryside and one of the founders of the National Trust, who wrote at the turn of the century:

'Let the grass growing for hay be respected, let the primrose roots be left in their loveliness in the hedges, the birds unmolested and the gates shut. If those who frequented country places would consider those who live there, they would better deserve, and more often retain, the rights and privileges they enjoy.'

* * *

Eastbourne Pier at the start of the South Downs Way

THE SOUTH DOWNS WAY

THE SOUTH DOWNS WAY

Opened in 1972 to run initially for eighty-odd miles between Beachy Head and Buriton, the South Downs Way was the first officially designated long distance path to be developed as bridleway throughout its entire length. In one or two places the bridleway and footpath routes diverge but, apart from the initial stage from Eastbourne to Alfriston, these are only modest alternatives and by far the major part of the Way is shared by ramblers and horse riders (and cyclists).

No matter how attractive the village of Buriton near the Sussex-Hampshire border might be, it has always been rather an unsatisfactory, low-key finish to a long-distance walk, while Winchester offers a more obvious goal - the cathedral marking a natural finalé to a pilgrimage along the Downs. In recognition of this attempts were made over several years to have the route officially extended as far as Winchester, and in November 1987 the Countryside Commission sent its proposals for this extension to the Secretary of State for the Environment for his approval. The route described in this guide is that suggested by the Countryside Commission and now approved.

For the greater part of its length the route follows along the northern crest of the South Downs escarpment, with broad views over the low Wealden farmlands in one direction, and the rolling Downs in the other. Nestling between downland hills to the south are the clefts of dry valleys, called Bottoms, or Deans. Beyond them in the eastern sector gleams the English Channel, but farther west the nature of the Downs changes and there is less a sense of height and space, and the sea is all but a memory.

There are only a few steep ascents and descents to be made where the five rivers (Cuckmere, Ouse, Adur and Arun in Sussex, and the Meon in Hampshire) have cut their broad valleys through the chalk. Mostly, though, the route remains along the crest, sometimes along clear trackways, sometimes on flint paths, sometimes on the soft luxury of turf. For much of the way the path remains above 650 feet. In the eastern half the Downs are open and exposed, but towards Hampshire woodlands become more frequent, but the quality of the path is almost always first-rate, stiles and gates well-maintained, waymarking superb.

History is ever-present on this walk, for the crests of the Downs were long ago used by nomadic tribes as convenient highways above

the dense forests and mire of the Weald. Neolithic man began to culti-
vate them and mine for flint. In the Bronze Age and Iron Age
primitive farm sites, long barrows and hill forts began to pepper the
ridges, and their tell-tale signs are there to this day - although modern
farming practices have destroyed evidence of many in recent years.
Along the route of the South Downs Way there are something like 400
Bronze Age burial burrows. There are lynchets (ancient field systems)
dating from the Iron Age, rippling the grass slopes where ploughed
land long ago slipped against the original small field boundaries of
piled stone. (At Butser Hill, south of Petersfield, will be found one of
many Iron Age sites of habitation and cultivation including three
defensive dykes, lynchets, burial mounds and ancient trackways. On
land now managed by Hampshire County Council the Butser Ancient
Farm Research Centre carries out interesting experiments using crops,
methods, materials and livestock similar to those known by Iron Age
farmers. Our route passes alongside the demonstration site.)

During the Roman occupation routes of trade and communication
were engineered across the South Downs, and so advanced were their
methods of construction that many have been adopted as modern
rights of way. In places the long-distance walker of today uses tracks
that were laid in the first century B.C., and west of Bignor Hill the
South Downs Way comes to a large wooden signpost bearing
directions to *Noviomagus* and *Londinium* (Chichester and London) on
the line of the Roman Stane Street - built around 70 A.D. (Half an
hour's walk away are the remains of Bignor Roman Villa; nearer to the
Way are the earthworks of a Stone Age causewayed camp.)

History is all around us on the Downs.

* * *

Which way to walk? West to east, or east to west? There are argu-
ments to favour either approach. Winchester makes an obvious goal,
but the scenic grandeur of Beachy Head and the Seven Sisters is
thought by many to be the highlight of the walk and best left 'til last.
Most of our weather comes from the west, so it might be thought
preferable to walk eastwards, so to have the wind behind you; yet if a
cold easterly is blowing it would be better to head west with the
rucksack's protection.

This guide offers directions for both ways. The main text follows the
route westwards, but an alternative description is given for the east-
bound walker too.

The route begins near Beachy Head outside Eastbourne. There is an

19

initial divergence of ways, for the bridleway heads inland via Jevington whilst the footpath goes along the clifftop of the Seven Sisters as far as the Cuckmere Valley, then north above the valley to Alfriston. The two routes join here.

From Alfriston the South Downs Way climbs to Firle Beacon and only descends from the escarpment through necessity to cross the valley cut by the River Ouse. On then to Mill Hill, Iford Hill and Swanborough Hill; across the A27 and onto Balmer Down which leads to a splendid section with broad views over the Weald. Ditchling Beacon is invariable busy with day trippers. Then we descend to Pyecombe before climbing again, soon to come to Devil's Dyke and, keeping high, cross a series of hills. After the last of these, Truleigh Hill, the route loses a lot of height in order to cross the River Adur below Steyning.

West of the Adur Chanctonbury Ring is the major landmark; an historic circle of beech trees that sadly suffered in the great gale that hit southern England in October 1987. The busy A24 is crossed near Washington, then up onto the Downs again with more broad vistas and a few woodlands. Then the River Arun forces another break of stride, but after the village of Houghton it is back to the hills again. This time, though, the Downs are becoming more wooded and a long stretch of broad-leaved tree shade takes us across Cocking Down.

Philliswood Down follows and Sussex gives way to Hampshire. Buriton, once the end of the walk, now lies a little north of the route and we continue along the Downs to pass through the expanse of Queen Elizabeth Forest, (where there's every possibility of catching sight of deer) and immediately afterwards wander beside Butser Ancient Farm. Butser Hill demands a stiff climb, but thereafter follows a stretch of country lane walking which in turn leads to a long track across Tegdown Hill and beside woods to the inland naval establishment of HMS Mercury.

More downland tracks lead to historic Old Winchester Hill, now a National Nature Reserve on the site of an Iron Age hill fort. Here the bridleway and footpath part company for a while, but join forces again in the valley of the lovely little River Meon at Exton. A last stage takes us from this village onto Beacon Hill (another Nature Reserve), then by one or two lanes to cross the route of the Wayfarer's Walk, and on tracks that lead to lonely Gander Down and Cheesefoot Head. Telegraph Hill is next, within earshot of rifle ranges, and the map is red with Danger Areas. But our route leads down a sunken track in safety to the attractive hamlet of Chilcomb which is just one long field away from Winchester.

A maze of streets takes the South Downs Way through the eastern part of town, over the River Itchen to King Alfred's fine statue, and into the gounds of Winchester Cathedral where the peace of centuries is held in trust; a fitting end to a walk through the peace of the South Downs landscape.

*   *   *

SOUTH DOWNS WAY - WEST BOUND (EASTBOURNE TO WINCHESTER)

SECTION 1:   **EASTBOURNE TO ALFRISTON**
                         (via The Seven Sisters)

Distance:	12 miles
Map:	O.S. Landranger series; Sheet 199 *Eastbourne, Hastings & Surrounding Area* 1:50,000
Accommodation:	Eastbourne - Hotels, b&b, Youth Hostel (Beachy Head)
	Alfriston - Hotels, b&b, Youth Hostel

Of the two primary stages leading to Alfriston, this route across Beachy Head and the Seven Sisters is not a bridleway, but is the official walkers' route. The bridleway alternative goes inland via Jevington and is described as Section 1(a) below. It is difficult to say which is the finer route, for both have much to commend them. This clifftop path is a dramatic one for the surf froths far below and as you wander across Beachy Head a lovely view is given ahead to the Seven Sisters and Seaford Head beyond the estuary of Cuckmere Haven. The inland route makes a splendid introduction to the Downs, for there are wide open views almost every step of the way, and the little community of Jevington is a typical flint-walled downland village with an attractive church. It is tempting to recommend you walk both stages in due course.

The official route begins on the southern outskirts of Eastbourne at Holy-well. It then wanders up steps and onto the scrub-lively cliffs to Beachy Head, continues across to Birling Gap and onto the successive rise and fall of the Seven Sisters. After Haven Brow, the last of the 'Sisters', the route drops to the east bank of the Cuckmere River and follows this northward as

21

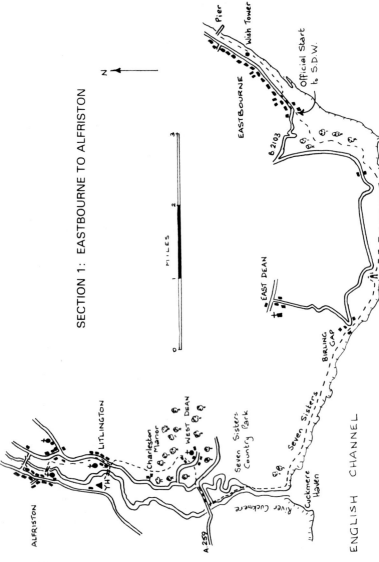

SECTION 1: EASTBOURNE TO ALFRISTON

far as Exceat Bridge. A short stretch of road walking, then steeply up a grassy hillside to Friston Forest. Straight through this, down to West Dean and back into forest again. Trees are traded for a high farmland path leading to Litlington and soon after you come to Alfriston.

Refreshments are available at Beachy Head, Birling Gap, Exceat Bridge and Litlington.

* * *

The actual start to the South Downs Way is rather insignificant for both the Seven Sisters route and the inland alternative, and it would be much more satisfactory to begin on the very sea shore. This description, then, starts beside Eastbourne Pier (1). (Grid ref: 617989)

Facing the Channel turn right and wander south-westwards along the promenade towards a stumpy Martello Tower (2) known as the Wish Tower. Beyond it are neat lawns and flower beds. The promenade continues alongside these towards the rising cliffs for a third of a mile or so. As the path rises and comes to a large landscaped mound with seats placed around it, bear right to King Edward's Parade. (The two routes divide here.)

Head to the left to Holywell, and on coming to a refreshment kiosk you will find the first South Downs Way sign. A notice board nearby gives information about the route. Head up a flight of steps and then on a well-worn path. At a junction of tracks, take the left-hand option through gorse, raspberry canes and scrub, coming out onto open downland above the rim of Whitbread Hole and its playing field. The continuing path winds through bushes of blackthorn, gorse and elder around Heathy Brow and then, climbing steadily on an old coastguard's path and with splendid views over the sea, approaches Beachy Head (3). *(Refreshments)*

Continue along the clifftop (but do not stray too close to the edge as the cliffs are liable to crumble away) which descends almost to road level below the former lighthouse at Belle Tout, then climbs to pass round the inland side of the wall that encloses it. Maintain direction across the cliffs, which were acquired by the National Trust in 1967, pass a coastguard station and slope down to the buildings and car park at Birling Gap. *(Refreshments)*

I was glad then to have chosen to walk westwards, for although the sky was bright and clear a cold easterly wind was blowing, and I'd rather have that in my back than in my face all day. On the clifftop walk there were tiny cowslips coming into bloom, but few other flowers. Later, and farther inland, there would be plenty of colour around my boots, but up here I was

23

well content with views over the sea, the bleached helter-skelter of the Seven Sisters ahead with their thatch of downland grass, and recalled previous wanderings along them at the end of other long walks. Despite the fact that there will always be others walking along these cliffs - families out for a short stroll, others exercising their dogs, determined ramblers striding across the turf - the pleasure of wandering across the Seven Sisters never palls. There's the cry of gulls, the sight, scent and sound of the sea, and broad vistas of the Downs stretching far away inland. It was good to be back.

A flint track leads ahead to the right of the buildings and goes inland for a few paces, then you bear left over grass to rejoin the clifftop once more. The route now wanders over the Seven Sisters on a switchback course with the sea glistening below to the left and the green of the Downs spreading far off to the right. The first of these cliffs (or 'Sisters') is Went Hill. Next is Bailey's Hill, followed by Flagstaff Point, Brass Point, Rough Brow, Short Brow and Haven Brow. After Haven Brow, so-called for its view overlooking Cuckmere Haven, the route leads down and curves slightly to the right on a chalk track which leads to a fence and a stile. Over this follow along a grassy embankment which forms the east bank of the Cuckmere River, and stay with it as far as Exceat Bridge. *(Refreshments)* Now turn right alongside the busy A259 a short distance to reach Exceat Farm which now houses the headquarters of the Seven Sisters Country Park (4).

Just beyond the barn a stile on the left gives access to a steep meadow, at the top of which a stone stile leads through a low wall and onto the edge of Friston Forest (5). Take the path ahead through the trees, soon to descend a flight of more than 200 steps to the hamlet of West Dean (6), which you reach beside a most attractive duck pond. Cross the road and continue ahead to pass Forge Cottage on your left along a concrete track. On re-entering Friston Forest take the first track on the left. On coming to a T junction turn right, and when the track bears sharp right near the edge of the forest, cross a stile and descend another flight of wood-braced steps among more trees to the edge of the grounds of Charleston Manor (7).

The South Downs Way continues ahead and climbs a slope, crosses a stile and follows the line of a hedge, still heading north. (On the downland slopes to the west, on the far side of the Cuckmere Valley, can be seen a horse carved in the chalk.) The path leads without difficulty to Litlington *(refreshments)*. From Exceat Bridge to this village we have been sharing the route of the Vanguard Way (8).

Note: *For walkers planning to stay overnight at Alfriston Youth Hostel, you are advised to leave the South Downs Way in Litlington. Just after the village pub, The Plough and Harrow, take a path to the left which will* *lead to a bridge crossing the Cuckmere. Go up the slope beyond, and the Youth Hostel is the building immediately on the right beside the road.*

Turn right in the village street and continue ahead past The Plough and Harrow. A short distance beyond the church of St. Michael's an enclosed path on the left of the road leads the route to the flint-walled Plonk Barn, converted to a private residence and standing on a blind bend in the narrow road. At this point the Seven Sisters route combines with the inland bridleway. Turn left opposite Plonk Barn along a footpath and cross the Cuckmere by a white-railed bridge. Alfriston church stands off to the left. On the west side of the river there's a choice of route: either continue straight ahead up an alleyway that leads directly into Alfriston's main street, where you turn right; or head to the right on a waymarked route in front of some cottages, then left between flint walls to reach the Market Cross in Alfriston High Street. Here bear left and walk along the street as far as the Star Inn.

Alfriston is seen as something of a show-piece village; certainly one of the busiest with day-trippers in all of Sussex. In its streets are many interesting and picturesque buildings, a number of them with typical downland flint walls. The 14th century church of St. Andrew is often called 'The Cathedral of the Downs'. Next door to it stands the Clergy House, a thatched, half-timbered house of similar vintage to the church. It was the first building acquired by the National Trust in 1896 - for £10! Among the many notable buildings in the main street there is the one-time smuggler's haunt of the George Inn (built 1397), and the Star Inn, which dates from the 15th century and bears the figurehead of a Dutch ship that foundered in Cuckmere Haven.

Things Seen On The Way:

1: *Eastbourne* is one of those grand South Coast resorts that retains its air of gentility at the expense of a younger generation. It's a town of flower beds and bowling greens, a town where Victorian imagery lingers on. The original settlement of East Bourne had a church before the Normans came. There were neighbouring hamlets called South Bourne and Sea Houses, a collection of fishermen's cottages. The three were combined in the mid-nineteenth century, and in 1910 Eastbourne was created a borough. Development of the town was due largely to the Duke of Devonshire and Carew Davies Gilbert.

2: *Martello Tower.* The Wish Tower on the promenade at Eastbourne is the sole survivor of four that were originally built along the seafront here in 1806/7 as a defence against Napoleon. During the

Napoleonic Wars a whole series of these stocky circular towers were erected along the coast of Sussex and Kent. They were named after the Torre della Martello in Napoleon's homeland of Corsica.

3: *Beachy Head* is one of the best-known features of the Sussex coast. The clifftop is 536 feet above the waves and the red and white lighthouse dwarfed below was built in 1902. Before its construction the nearest light was at nearby Belle Tout a little to the west, but standing on the clifftop its light was frequently lost in fog, so it was replaced by the sea-level tower we gaze down on today.

4: *Seven Sisters Country Park* occupies 690 acres of land east of the Cuckmere River. In the 18th century former barn at Exceat an exhibition hall has been established. The Centre is open daily to the public from Good Friday until the end of October, and at weekends in winter. Next to it another barn houses an exhibition of marine life.

5: *Friston Forest* covers almost 2,000 acres of mainly broad-leaved woodlands with conifer screening. It is leased by the Forestry Commission and there are several paths and rides through it, including the Vanguard Way, Forest Walk and Exceat Woodland Walk.

6: *West Dean* is an historic little place. It is said that Alfred the Great built a palace here in 850 AD, although no trace of one has been found. (Alfred is remembered all along the Cuckmere's windings.) But there is a rectory dating from the 13th century, and age seems to be in every corner of this tiny hamlet.

7: *Charleston Manor*, on the edge of Friston Forest, is a lovely Georgian building with Norman origins. It was mentioned in the Domesday Book. In the grounds stands a large 15th century tithe barn, 177 feet long, with an enormous tiled roof and a medieval circular dovecote. There are also fine stables two hundred years old. At certain times of the year the gardens are open to the public.

8: *The Vanguard Way* is a long distance walking route devised by the Vanguards Rambling Club, which leads in 62 miles from East Croydon in Surrey to Seaford Head. (Guidebooks: *The Wealdway & The Vanguard Way* by Kev Reynolds (Cicerone Press); *The Vanguard Way* written and published by The Vanguards Rambling Club.)

Accommodation:

Eastbourne   Numerous hotels and guest-houses. For official guidebook write to the Tourist Information Centre, 3 Cornfield Terrace, BN21 4NW. Tel: E/B 27474

Beachy Head Youth Hostel, East Dean Road,
BN20 8ES. Tel: E/B 21081
Mr. & Mrs. J.Dove, Strathleven, 17 South Cliff Ave.
BN20 7AH. Tel: E/B 23016
Mrs. M.Norman, Gley-Roy, 75 Pevensey Road,
BN21 3HS. Tel: E/B 31389

Alfriston   Youth Hostel, Frog Firle, Alfriston, Polegate,
BN26 5TT. Tel: Alfriston 870423
Riverdale Private Hotel, Seaford Road, Alfriston,
Polegate, BN26 5TR. Tel: Alfriston 870397
Mrs. D.Savage, Pleasant Rise Farm, Alfriston,
Polegate, BN26 5TN. Tel: Alfriston 870545
Star Inn, Alfriston, Polegate, BN26 5TA.
Tel: Alfriston 870495

Public Transport:
Eastbourne is served by British Rail (London via Lewes or Hastings).
Buses run to *Beachy Head*, *Exceat* and *Alfriston*.

SECTION 1(a):   **EASTBOURNE TO ALFRISTON**
                  (Inland route via Jevington)

Distance:	9 miles
Map:	O.S. Landranger series; Sheet 199 *Eastbourne, Hastings & Surrounding Area* 1:50,000
Accommodation:	Eastbourne - Hotels, b&b, Youth Hostel (Beachy Head)
	Alfriston - Hotels, b&b, Youth Hostel

This alternative to the Seven Sisters route is bridleway throughout (other than the initial section along Eastbourne promenade which is not officially part of the South Downs Way). It is a lovely stage of rolling downland with wide views and plenty of interest all the way. In many respects it is as fine as the official footpath route already described, albeit of a completely different nature, and is highly recommended.
   As with the Seven Sisters route it is considered more appropriate to begin

our long walk on the seafront at Eastbourne - especially as the official start in an untidy corner off Paradise Road is such an unspectacular beginning to what is destined to be a journey of many scenic pleasures. Once on the route proper we emerge onto the Downs near a golf course with views over the town and off to the flat acres of the Pevensey Levels, and head north before descending a clear track to the first narrow valley with the village of Jevington neatly spaced within it. A tree-shaded climb leads onto the Downs again, and at Windover Hill we walk above the unseen head of England's largest chalk figure, the Long Man of Wilmington. More big views look across the Cuckmere's gap towards Bostal Hill and Firle Beacon, and northward into the depths of the Weald.

A winding track takes us down to the Cuckmere's valley, then along a narrow lane as far as Plonk Barn where we join the Seven Sisters route for the last short stroll into Alfriston.

Refreshments are available in Jevington.

✶ ✶ ✶

From Eastbourne Pier (1) (Grid ref: 617989) to King Edward's Parade the route is the same as that for the alternative stage already described. Having symbolically greeted the English Channel by the pier, turn right and head south-westwards along the promenade towards the stumpy Martello Tower (2) known as Wish Tower. Continue beyond it to walk past neat lawns and flower beds and with the cliffs rising ahead. About a third of a mile or so beyond Wish Tower the surfaced path rises to a large landscaped mound with seats placed around it. Two or three paths merge here. Turn right and a few paces later reach King Edward's Parade.

Cross over into Chesterfield Road and wander along this residential street to the far end where you bear right. Now walk along Milnthorpe Road, over St. John's Road and then straight ahead along Gaudick Road. When you come to the end of Gaudick Road cross half-left ahead into Paradise Road, and soon after Link Road breaks away to the left. Ignoring this continue ahead and in a few yards you come to a sign announcing the official start to the South Downs Way. (Grid ref: 597981)

The slopes of Pashley Down rise ahead and you wander up the bridleway with a brief woodland of ilex and beech on the right. Half hidden among the trees near the bridleway is a domed reservoir looking like something out of a sci-fi movie. Soon there are views behind overlooking the town; the sea gleams to a far horizon, and before long the way leads onto the edge of the Downs with a fence

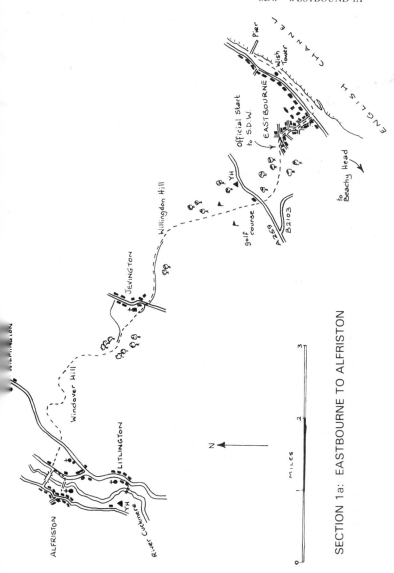

SECTION 1a: EASTBOURNE TO ALFRISTON

Jevington from the South Downs Way

ahead. Bear right and wander along a grass track above trees and scrub, with impressive views over Eastbourne. The vague trail leads to the A259 (Brighton-Eastbourne road) with the clubhouse of East-bourne Downs Golf Club opposite, and the golf course stretching beyond.

Note: *Beachy Head Youth Hostel is situated about a third of a mile downhill. Turn right and walk down the roadside footpath. The hostel, which occupies the former golf clubhouse, stands back on the left a few paces from the road. Next to it is the official end to The Wealdway long-distance path.*

Cross the road and take the stony track directly ahead. A South Downs Way marker stone is seen beside the track. The way leads through the golf course (views over Pevensey Levels) and when this finishes continue in the same direction, sometimes on grass, then along a rutted track. There are fine views almost all the way. You will pass a concrete dew pond (3) and soon after the trig point on Willingdon Hill. (The mound which marks this hill once bore a wind-mill.) Just beyond this you come to cross tracks and some interesting stone markers (4). (The track heading to the right is part of The Wealdway (5).) Ignoring routes to right and left continue ahead, descending a fence-enclosed track with a lovely view of Jevington in its hollow below.

True downland spread in gentle curves on all sides. Pausing to take it all in I recognised the shape of Combe Hill to the north where I had crossed one glorious late-spring afternoon a couple of years ago when walking the Wealdway. I remembered it well; the peace, the views, the sunshine. Now I had the peace of a spring morning, more fine views and sunshine too. Ahead, Jevington sank into a fold of hills. Behind it a sloping meadow on the Downs had been recently rolled in strips, as though a welcome carpet had been laid out for my arrival. In one such meadow horses were grazing; in another the lazy drift of sheep shuffled patterns of white on green. Happiness, I thought, is something we're seldom aware of until it has passed. Wandering down the track towards Jevington that morning with the sun on my neck, I knew there was nowhere else I'd rather be, and nothing I'd rather be doing than setting off on a hundred-mile walk along those Downs. Ambling down the track to Jevington, I was happy. And knew it.

The track to Jevington (6) is a flowery one; cowslips, bugle, wild raspberry canes straggling by the fence. On reaching the village turn right on the road and a few paces later go left on the approach to the church. *(For refreshments, continue along the village street beyond the turning for the church, to find the Eight Bells pub.)*

Continue past the Saxon church of St. Andrew *(the trim April grass in the graveyard a-speckle of white and blue - daisies, forget-me-knots and bluebells)* along a narrowing enclosed track. A signpost indicates Alfriston 3 miles. When the left-hand fence finishes the path climbs the hillside among horse chestnut and elder. Cross another track, and shortly after you will come onto a broad farm track where you bear left and continue up the slope. (Wild garlic and bluebells growing among the trees on either side in spring.) At Holt Brow the track emerges from tree shade and the South Downs Way breaks off to the right on a grassy path among scrub, and a few paces later comes to a pair of bridle gates leading into a large open meadow.

There is a sudden awareness of space as you come onto the bare crest of the Downs. There are far-off views to the sea on the left. Nearer, the meadows fold into the green combe of Deep Dean. To the right a fence is lined with gorse and ahead, on the far side of the fence the ruined walls of Hill Barn gives rise to speculation as to their origins.

More or less maintaining direction across this pasture, keeping Deep Dean well to your left, continue ahead. Then, when you are just beyond the northern lip of the combe, you come to the edge of the escarpment and veer left to go through a gate. (Grid ref: 544033) The crest here is quite narrow and views to the north are both extensive

Jevington Church

and appealing. Way below lies the little village of Wilmington. Beyond that lies Arlington Reservoir and the immense levels of the Weald. The Cuckmere River may be seen snaking out of the Weald, and to the west you gaze across the broad valley it has eaten through the Downs, to the rise of Bostal Hill and Firle Beacon where the route passes on Section 2.

Immediately below, unseen from this cowslip-yellow crest, is the Long Man of Wilmington (7) which is such a feature of the South Downs. The chalk path leading to it can be seen quite clearly cutting through the meadows from the village. This path too, is a part of the Wealdway long-distance route.

Continue ahead through the gate, now heading south-west on a grassy trail and passing along the left-hand side of various earthworks on Windover Hill (two or three burial barrows and ditches, and mounds that indicate refuse pits from Stone Age flint mines). *(Our boots tread paths of an ancient history; we follow in the footsteps of the first Sussex Downsmen, on the very same Downs - but how different were the landscapes they gazed upon?)*

Beyond the summit of Windover Hill the route winds to the right, then left, descending round the head of another combe, Ewe Dean, with the northern slopes of the Downs plunging dramatically away to

32

the Cuckmere's valley. The track leads past an underground reservoir and comes to a narrow country lane. (This leads from Wilmington to Litlington.) Cross straight over and continue down a narrow sunken track among blackthorn and under a line of elms, until you emerge at a road junction.

Note: *The official South Downs Way route turns left here and follows the narrow lane to Plonk Barn before heading across the Cuckmere River into Alfriston. A better alternative for walkers - this is not a bridleway - would be to take the road directly ahead for a few yards to the hump-backed bridge over the river, and then follow a footpath heading left on either bank as far as Alfriston.*

For the South Downs Way proper turn left and walk along the narrow lane (taking care of traffic) for about 400 yards until you come to Plonk Barn, a converted barn on a bend in the road. Turn right onto a footpath, joining the Seven Sisters route, and cross a white-railed bridge over the Cuckmere with Alfriston church seen off to the left. Over the bridge either keep straight ahead along an alleyway leading into Alfriston High Street, or bear right in front of some cottages, then left between flint walls to reach the Market Cross in the High Street. Now head left along the street as far as the Star Inn.

Note: *For those planning to stay overnight at the Youth Hostel, the most pleasant route is to follow the riverside footpath - on the left bank - downstream as far as Litlington. Then cross the footbridge and walk up the slope to a road where the hostel is the flint-walled building immediately on the right.*

(For details about Alfriston, see end of Section 1 above.)

Thinks Seen On The Way:

1: *Eastbourne* owes it prosperity to development by the Duke of Devonshire and Carew Davies Gilbert. It has an elegant, Victorian charm; a resort of flower gardens and bowling greens set below the towering cliffs of Beachy Head.

2: *Martello Tower.* Officially, Martello Tower number 73, but also known as Wish Tower, this is one of a number of similar defensive forts built along the Kent and Sussex coast during the Napoleonic Wars when Britain feared invasion. These thick, brick-built circular towers were named after Torre della Martello in Corsica.

3: *Dew Ponds* are seen in a number of places along the South Downs. Because of the permeable nature of chalk, there is practically no natural surface water on the Downs, so saucer-shaped scoops have been dug out and given a base of concrete (clay was originally used) to trap and contain rain water.

4: *Willingdon Hill Stone Markers*. At cross tracks on Willingdon Hill will be seen curious stone direction signs bearing strange markings. One indicates the route to Jevington beside the continuing route. Originally these were part of the Barclays Bank building in Eastbourne that was bombed during the last war.

5: *The Wealdway* is a long-distance route which leads in 82 miles from the banks of the Thames in Gravesend, Kent, to the clifftop of Beachy Head. A fine, ever-varied walk that crosses the North Downs, High Weald ridges, Ashdown Forest, the expanse of the Weald itself and, finally, the South Downs. (Guidebook: *The Wealdway & The Vanguard Way* by Kev Reynolds (Cicerone Press).)

6: *Jevington* is a quiet, back-valley downland hamlet that was once a smugglers' haunt. The small church of St. Andrew has an impressive Saxon tower 1,000 years old. The remainder of the church dates from the 13th century, but there are Roman bricks in its construction. The tower contains a bell brought ashore from a shipwreck.

7: *The Long Man of Wilmington* is England's largest chalk figure. He stands 226 feet long with a stave in each hand and overlooks the ruins of a Benedictine priory on the edge of Wilmington village. No-one knows the Long Man's origins, but there have been plenty of theories. A plaque near his feet describes some of these theories. He rests in the care of the Sussex Archaeological Trust, who also look after Wilmington Priory.

Accommodation:
For accommodation in Eastbourne and Alfriston, refer to details at the end of Section 1 above.

Public Transport:
Eastbourne is served by British Rail (London via Lewes or Hastings). Buses run to *Alfriston*.

SECTION 2: **ALFRISTON TO RODMELL**

Distance:	8 miles
Maps:	O.S. Landranger series; Sheet 199 *Eastbourne, Hastings & Surrounding Area* and 198 *Brighton &*

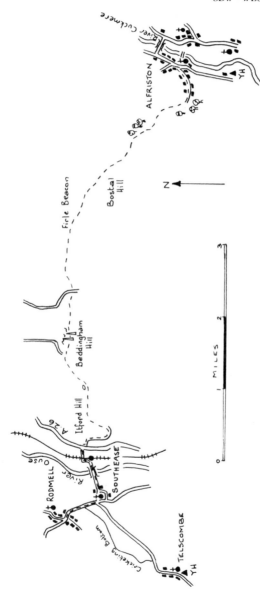

SECTION 2:   ALFRISTON TO RODMELL

	The Downs 1:50,000
Accommodation:	Rodmell - Guest-house, b&b
	Elsewhere - Youth Hostel at Telscombe (2 miles off route)

This is a lovely walk along the northern crest of the Downs; a walk on downland grass lush with flowers, among numerous sites of ancient history where long barrows roughen the turf. We pass a Saxon cemetery remote today from the world of men - apart, that is, from South Downs Way walkers and farmers about their isolated business. We share the lonely hills with sheep and wander a belvedere course with those constant broad vistas around us.

From Alfriston's busy heart the route takes us up to Bostal Hill and just beyond where hang-gliders imitate the soaring birds. Then on to Firle Beacon, 713 feet above the sea, in a land cropped smooth by generations of sheep. The Downs then curve westwards and we cross Beddingham Hill beside a pair of lofty radio masts, and come to Itford Hill overlooking the breach in the Downs made by the River Ouse. Down we go to cross the river into a tiny hamlet with the contented name of Southease. There then follows a spell of road walking (happily a short spell) as far as Rodmell.

There are no prospects of refreshment at all along this section of the route. Southease is the only community between Alfriston and Rodmell, and that is too small to boast either a shop or a pub. Stock up with supplies before leaving Alfriston.

* * *

Walk along the narrow street leading down the side of the Star Inn which fronts onto Alfriston High Street. (Grid ref: 520031) In a few yards you come to a crossing road and go over this to continue ahead, walking uphill along a residential street. When the street deteriorates to a chalk and flint track bordered by ilex, continue up the slope. The track veers to the right still gaining height, then later, when it swings left, a lesser track branches off more or less ahead. Follow this on grass, over another track, and steadily climb up to the crown of the Downs passing a hidden long barrow (Long Burgh) and a Saxon burial ground. Once atop the Downs huge views take in the sea far out to the left. Behind, looking back on the previous section of the route, the Long Man of Wilmington is still hidden from view, but the rolling wall of downland is clearly seen above Wilmington and Alfriston, and stretching southward to Cuckmere Haven.

For a mile or more the clear flinty track leads along the very crest and then comes to a bridle gate beside a kissing gate. The broad green expanse beyond sweeps one's attention away to the right to the village of Berwick (a pretty corner) and the empty distances of the Weald; on the left to scooped combes and the sea.

Continue ahead across grass, then once again on a more obvious track over Bostal Hill (624 feet) with a fence on your left. The slope takes you down to a small car park, which is popular with hang-gliding enthusiasts. (The narrow road to it leads from Bopeep Farm.) Wander straight ahead through some gates and pass a barn (in some disarray) on your right as you begin to climb the slope beyond on a rutted track. This leads directly to Firle Beacon, which is marked by a trig point. (Grid ref: 485059)

The way curves a little to the left now and heads westward with a pair of radio masts in view standing atop Beddingham Hill nearly two miles away. Our route actually goes right past them, so they form a convenient marker. Between Firle Beacon and Beddingham Hill the route goes through a hilltop car park, approached by road from West Firle (1) seen below at the foot of the Downs. (Radio-controlled model aircraft are often flown from here.)

Around us now are more prehistoric sites; round barrows and ancient settlements. There was an Iron Age village near Firle Beacon, a Bronze Age collection of huts and workshops west of Beddingham Hill. North of the escarpment, and on the outskirts of Glynde, there was an Iron Age hill fort on Mount Caburn. For more than 300 years it was occupied and active until the Romans came. Roman trackways crossed the Downs above West Firle as part of an important trade route. Grain would have been carted along these tracks bound for the coast where Seaford and Newhaven stand today. On these Downs, 'broad and bare to the skies' only a handful of modern cars, a few model aircraft and the twin radio masts ahead represent a world so different to that experienced by the first settlers of these green sweeping crests. Yet with imagination we can stir the spirits still of our windblown ancestors and share with them the empty miles.

Pass along the right-hand side of the radio masts. The track then veers a little to the right and goes through a gate by a narrow metalled road. Cross through another gate directly ahead and follow parallel with the left-hand fence towards Itford Hill, passing a trig point on a grassy bank containing the dried-up dew pond shown as Red Lion Pond on the map. (Grid ref: 446055) (This area is rich in wild flowers all the way to the valley of the Ouse.)

Coming to the brow of the hill Lewes is seen sprawling half-right ahead cupped by the Downs. Directly below to the west you will see a large farm on the side of the busy A26 road. This is Itford Farm and the route leads to it. Officially the way bears leftwards across the hillside (although there is little evidence on the ground) and then takes a chalk and flint track heading to the right. (This track is clearly seen from the brow of the hill.) It leads out to the main road. Bear right for a few paces, then cross the road with caution onto a narrow lane leading down the side of the farm. A signpost points to Southease.

The lane crosses a flat area of low meadows on its short journey to Southease on the right bank of the Ouse. Along the way it crosses the railway track at the halt of Southease station, then ahead over the tidal strip of the River Ouse, contained now between sturdy banks. Soon after you will enter the tiny, but attractive, hamlet of Southease (2) which consists of a few 17th century cottages, a pond, village green and lovely Norman church bearing a circular tower - so rare in Sussex.

Passing the church on your left, continue up the tree-lined lane to a road junction. Bear right onto the Newhaven to Lewes road and walk along it for half a mile to Rodmell.

Note: *Those intending to stay overnight at Telscombe's delightfully simple Youth Hostel should turn off this road, not at the first junction on the left, but just beyond it on a bridleway track. (This is about 250 yards after the road junction at Southease.) The track leads through the gentle vale of Cricketing Bottom, passing only a few farm buildings, then comes to a narrow lane. Go ahead on this and soon after you will enter the charming little hamlet of Telscombe. The Youth Hostel stands next to the church. Distance: about 2 miles from the Rodmell road.*

Rodmell is a small, somewhat straggling village overlooking the low-lying meadows that border the Ouse, but with the Downs rising to the west in a steady wall. The village has a Norman church and some attractive cottages. Virginia and Leonard Woolf lived here in Monks House. On the hill south-west of the village there once stood a windmill overlooking the gentle inner core of the Downs. There is a pub in Rodmell, the Abergavenny Arms, named after the Marquess of Avergavenny who was, until just after the First World War, the principal landowner. In the village there is limited bed and breakfast accommodation.

Things Seen On The Way:

1: *West Firle,* usually known simply as Firle, is a lovely compact little village nestling below the Downs. The elegant Firle Place, which stands near the church with a woodland behind it, was originally built in 1557, but then rebuilt nearly two hundred years later. It is open to the public.

2: *Southease* was a busy fishing village in Norman times when the

Telscombe Youth Hostel - a convenient overnight stop at the end of Section 2

River Ouse was a much more substantial waterway than today. Nowadays it has a quiet, almost lost air about it. The church is only one of three in Sussex to have a round tower. In it are a few murals dating from the 13th century.

Accommodation:

Rodmell	Mrs. Dean, Forge Guest-house, Rodmell, Lewes, BN7 3HS. Tel: Lewes 474740
	Mr. Fraser, Deep Thatch Cottage, Rodmell, Lewes, Tel: Lewes 477865
Telscombe	The Youth Hostel, Bank Cottages, Telscombe Lewes, BN7 3HZ. Tel: Brighton 37077

Public Transport:
Rodmell is served by bus (not Sundays) from Lewes and Newhaven. *Southease* has a rail link with Lewes, Newhaven and Seaford.

SECTION 3: **RODMELL TO NEWMARKET INN (A27)**

Distance:	5½ miles
Map:	O.S. Landranger series; Sheet 198 *Brighton & The Downs* 1:50,000
Accommodation:	None on route

This short stage takes us on a journey across another exposed broad downland ridge heading north-westward, first across Mill Hill, Front Hill and Iford Hill (not to be confused with Itford Hill on the last section), then along the scarp edge of Swanborough Hill overlooking neat villages tucked against the very feet of the Downs. Before cutting round Castle Hill we pass a spot where once stood Ashcombe Windmill; then on the line of a one-time track called Juggs Road used by fish traders travelling from Brighton to Lewes. Cold Combe swoops below, and the South Downs Way curves round its head and over the brow of Castle Hill before descending by the side of a little woodland known as Newmarket Plantation. It's all downhill then on to the A27 road at Newmarket Inn.

On a calm sunny day this is a gorgeous walk. Larks rise from the field to trill overhead. There will no doubt be pheasants and hares sharing your track if you walk quietly. There are badger setts along the edge of Swanborough Hill and foxes in Newmarket Plantation. And flowers smiling

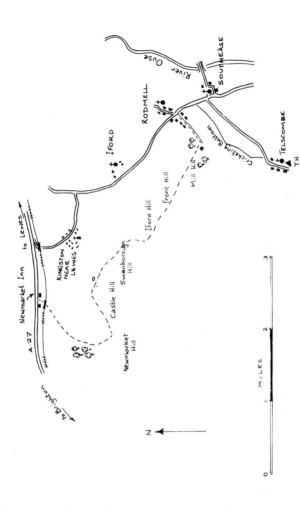

SECTION 3: RODMELL TO NEWMARKET INN

from the soft downland turf.

There are no refreshment facilities between Rodmell and the Newmarket Inn; indeed, there's no habitation at all after the last house on Mill Hill. But on reaching the A27 at Newmarket Inn there is a water tap for thirsty walkers beside the petrol station next to the inn.

* * *

Almost opposite the Abergavenny Arms in Rodmell, Mill Lane branches off to the left next to a small garage. Walk up this lane, initially between cottages. It then narrows and becomes a private road (but public bridleway) with fields on the left folding down into Cricketing Bottom. Near the crest of Mill Hill, and by the entrance drive to a house, lovely views are shown out towards the sea. Seaford Head can be seen far off to the left.

The South Downs Way bridleway now breaks away to the right here along a narrow enclosed track that suddenly opens to a spacious landscape with the track clearly seen forging ahead, and guided by a fence on the right. For a little over a mile and a half the route follows a steady course over the typical farmed downland scenery of Front Hill and Iford Hill. It is wide open country here. Open to the breezes, open to the sun. You pass through one or two bridle gates, then step along a concrete farm road with big fields on either side.

Mid-morning April sun beamed down and washed my shadow into the young spring corn. Out of that flint-cluttered corn rose one lark after another, thrashing the air with their wings, they sang as they soared higher and higher intent on distracting my attention away from their nests. What a gift for a solitary walker! Then over the brow of the hill ahead came three track-suited athletes chatting as they ran. (Lord knows where they found the breath to talk. Lord knows where they'd started from.) Within a matter of moments they were past me and pounding the concrete on the downhill slope to Mill Hill. I was glad when they had disappeared from sight, for this was a landscape that needed no human interruption. These Downs belonged to the birds and animals. Alone, one could absorb their strengths and their frailties, their past and their present, their own personal songs and scents. Alone, one could share their secrets and be glad for the day. I was well content to be on my own.

After a very long straight stretch of concrete the farm road veers sharply to the left towards a large barn. Leave the road at this bend and head off to the right for about 60 yards, then go through a gate into a sloping meadowland. Turn left and walk along the top edge of the slope which sweeps steeply down in corrugations of sheep tracks towards the little village of Iford, whose church is a real gem. This is a truly pleasant stretch to walk along, one of the best for many a long mile, for the eye is constantly being drawn down the flanks of the hills, rucked here and there by steep combes, to the villages of Iford and Kingston near Lewes, with the substantial buildings of Swanborough Manor (dating from the 12th century) in between. One or two paths rise up the slope, and at a point where the crest narrows to give a view left into a splendid combe, a bridleway crosses the South Downs Way. This is Breach Road which links Kingston near Lewes with Rottingdean. Shortly after this you pass through a gate onto a broad grassy hilltop.

There is little sign of track here, but maintain direction to pass to the left of Kingston Hill dewpond, (Grid ref: 383078) then veer slightly leftwards to another dewpond by a gate where Ashcombe Windmill used to spin its six sweeps (or sails) to the wind. You are now on the line of Juggs Road (1), although there's little to show for it on the ground.

Pass through the gate and head south-westwards keeping parallel with a fence on your right. Beyond the fence the scarp slope dips towards the traffic-mad A27 a mile and a world away. Contrast that with the cowslips at your feet and the song of the larks high above! Near the end of this long meadow veer leftwards to find a bridle gate and a stile. Beyond these turn half-right and follow the right-hand fence. It leads to another bridle gate which you go through and descend the slope with a fence now on your left. Off to the right you peer across Cold Combe, and as you near the foot of the slope so you enjoy a clear view of this fine rich downland.

Newmarket Plantation, a beechwood badly hit by the storm of October 16th 1987, stands on your left. A track leads past it, goes through two or three more gates, passes beneath a railway arch and emerges beside the Lewes to Brighton road between a petrol station and the Newmarket Inn. (Grid ref: 379091)

Lewes, the county town, is less than two miles away to the right. In the town there should be plenty of accommodation. There are shops, restaurants, Post Office, banks, chemists etc. Brighton is 6 miles down the road to the left.

Things Seen On The Way:

1: *Juggs Road* is a one-time trading route crossing the South Downs and used by fisher-folk from Brighton. 'Juggs' was the name given to these traders by the people of Lewes. They regularly carted their fish by donkey along this route to market in the county town. There is practically no sign of it on the section of our walk, although we follow its alignment between Kingston Hill and Newmarket Hill.

Accommodation:
None available along this Section, but there are hotels, guest-houses and b&b in Lewes. (2 miles) Information and lists from: Lewes Information Centre, Lewes House, 32 High Street, Lewes, BN7 2LX. Tel: Lewes 471600.

Public Transport:
Buses pass *Newmarket Inn* bound for Lewes and Brighton. *Falmer* (2 miles west along the Brighton road) has rail links with Brighton, Lewes and Eastbourne.

SECTION 4:   **NEWMARKET INN TO PYECOMBE**

Distance:	8½ miles
Map:	O.S. Landranger series; Sheet 198 *Brighton & The Downs* 1:50,000
Accommodation:	None on route, but at-
	Ditchling - b&b (2 miles off route)
	Hassocks - Hotel (1½ miles off route)
	Patcham - Youth Hostel (2½ miles off route)

Between the summer madness of the A27 outside Lewes and the A23 at Pyecombe the South Downs reward with birdsong and the bleating of sheep. Much of this stretch of countryside has been put to the plough. Arable has replaced pasture, but around Ditchling Beacon, one of the highest points on our route, the Downs are protected as Nature Reserve and the grasslands are much as they would have been for centuries. Wide views become commonplace. But earlier, in a 'back-country' of folded hills blocked by woodland crowns, one loses all sense of height and spaciousness as we stroll between large fields with no plunging scarp slope to draw perspective.

It's another historic area with a number of ancient sites along the way. During the first part of the walk from the Newmarket Inn the track passes to the west of flower-rich Mount Harry where, in 1264, Simon de Montfort fought Henry III in the Battle of Lewes which led to our present Parliamentary system. On Plumpton Plain there's the site of a Bronze Age settlement; in Ditchling village, the Romans had a fortified camp. (Stretches of Roman road may still be detected traversing west-east below

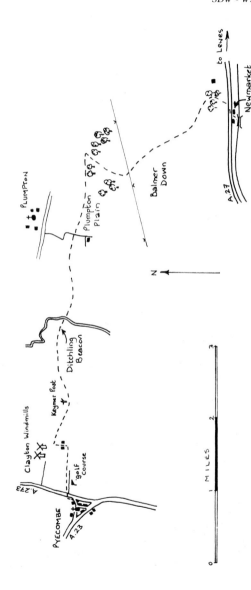

SECTION 4: NEWMARKET INN TO PYECOMBE

45

the Downs.)

On a winding track from the busy dual carriageway we soon trade traffic noise for the stillness of the Downs. Through a little wood and out to a bowl of fields, then walking straight along a gentle rise we come to woods, skirt them and suddenly find oursleves on the rim of the Downs once more, gazing north into the toyland of the Weald. Heading west then, with views all the way, we come to Ditchling Beacon, highest part of the South Downs Way in Sussex, where the walker will seldom find solitude. Less than two miles later a pair of windmills rise out of the fields ahead. These are Jack and Jill, the well-known Clayton Windmills. The way skirts these to the south, follows a track alongside a scenic golf course, and comes onto the main road a short stroll from the little traffic-marooned village of Pyecombe.

There are no refreshment facilities between Newmarket Inn and Pyecombe, other than an ice-cream van which is usually to be found in the car park at Ditchling Beacon. A water tap is situated at the start of the walk beside the petrol station next to Newmarket Inn.

* * *

Cross the dual carriageway with due caution, bear right for a few yards and then go up the clear path on the left to a bridle gate and stile. The way climbs easily and comes to a little wood next to a long flint wall containing the grounds of a Georgian mansion, Ashcombe House. Go through a gate and walk along the narrow track which leads through Ashcombe Wood (or Ashcombe Plantation), a rather scrubby woodland but lavish with wild flowers in spring.

Unseen, a cuckoo gave a hoarse hiccup of a call from somewhere ahead to the right. He was answered by another behind me. To and fro, like a verbal see-saw, their monotonous (yet thrilling) up-down messages flowed over the treetops. A wren flashed ahead of me on the path, stopped to curse my intrusion, then darted away again. But what really held my attention as I wandered among the storm-battered sycamores, were the shade-loving flowers beside the path and clustered around the forlorn tilted trunks that had been scythed by 1987's autumn gale. What might otherwise have been a sad remnant of a wood had been transformed into a natural garden of plenty, and I rejoiced again at my good fortune in having the opportunity to experience it.

On the far side of the wood a series of folding hills formed a complicated landscape. Cross the sloping meadow ahead to a bridle gate, then half-left along the edge of a field guided by a fence on the right. After passing through another gate the way maintains direction, this time though, the fence is on the left.

There follows a lengthy stretch as you rise gently up the arable slopes of Balmer Down without diverting from your course for about two miles. Shortly after walking beneath a line of power cables you will come to a crossing track and bear right along it, passing a hilltop wood on the left and then to continue between hedges. Later, with the woods of Ashcombe Bottom spreading to the right and a smaller woodland to the left, turn sharply to the left along a clear farm track and soon find yourself on the edge of the escarpment.

The walk from here to Ditchling Beacon, about 2½ miles away, maintains a steady course along which you can enjoy the lovely Wealden panorama stretching far-off. Despite being on the crest of the Downs this first section is called Plumpton Plain. Then comes Streathill, Western Brow and Home Brow. The village of Plumpton is clearly seen below with the extensive buildings of its Agricultural College, the gleam of water at 16th century Plumpton Place and, farther to the north, the outline of Plumpton Racecourse.

Note: *Halfway along the track to Ditchling Beacon, the south Downs Way comes to a farm track heading away to the left to isolated Streathill Farm. A mile and a half down this track is St. Mary's Farm, one of the few advertised camping sites along the route.*

On reaching the road at Ditchling Beacon (1) there's a busy unmade car park where an ice-cream van adds temptation for a brief rest. *(Walkers planning to stay overnight in Ditchling could attempt to hitch-hike down the road here.)* Cross through the car park, pass a little to the right of the trig point (813 feet) and follow the track through the Nature Reserve. The way is clear, sometimes over grassland, sometimes between fields, as it continues westward. A little over a mile from Ditchling Beacon you come to a tall wooden signpost with a carved acorn on top. This is known as the Keymer Post and it marks the boundary between East and West Sussex. (Unfortunately this post is a frequent target for vandalism.) Soon after passing this you catch your first sight of the Clayton Windmills (2).

Shortly before the windmills you come to a crossing track and turn left to walk to New Barn Farm. Continue between the farm buildings and 100 yards later, at cross tracks, head to the right along an enclosed path leading beside a golf course. This slopes downhill and comes onto the A273 Haywards Heath to Brighton road. Cross over, bear left along a narrow bush-lined path and walk into Pyecombe. Turn right into School Lane, then left along Church Lane in front of Pyecombe Church. This takes you down to the A23 beside the Plough Inn. (Grid ref: 292124)

Pyecombe is only a small village trapped in a wedge created by the A273

47

and A23. *The tapsell, or pintle, gate which leads into the churchyard here has a shepherd's crook as its latch. Pyecombe's fame arises from the manufacture of these shepherd's crooks which were used throughout the South Downs when great flocks populated the grassy slopes. The Norman church has an attractive 13th century tower and inside, a large lead font.*

Refreshments available at the Plough Inn which also serves meals.

Things Seen On The Way:

1: *Ditchling Beacon* is owned by the National Trust, with a Nature Reserve in the care of the Sussex Trust for Nature Conservation. From its 813 foot crown there is a noted panorama which, on a clear day, stretches to the North Downs across the Weald. The rectangular outline of an Iron Age hill fort surrounds the summit.

2: *The Clayton Windmills,* known as Jack and Jill, are a much-loved feature of the South Downs. Jack, the upper black-painted smock mill built in 1866, has been converted to a private residence while Jill, a gleaming white post mill, is in the care of a protection society and open to public inspection on Sundays between May and October. Jill originally stood in Brighton where she was built in 1821, but was towed onto the Downs by oxen to stand beside her masculine partner where she worked until 1909.

Accommodation:

Ditchling	Mrs. Adams, Beacon House, Beacon Road, Ditchling, Hassocks, BN6 8XB. Tel: Hassocks 4294
	Mrs. Bridges, Fyzabad, 51 Lewes Road, Ditchling, Hassocks, BN6 8SY. Tel: Hassocks 5136
Hassocks	Hassocks Hotel, Hassocks, BN6 8HN. Tel: Hassocks 2113
Patcham	The Youth Hostel, Patcham Place, Brighton, BN1 8YD. Tel: Brighton 556196

Public Transport:

Pyecombe is on a bus route to Brighton (for Patcham Y.H.) and Horsham.

Jack, the larger of the two Clayton windmills

SECTION 5:   **PYECOMBE TO BOTOLPHS (Adur Valley)**

Distance:	7½ miles
Map:	O.S. Landranger series; Sheet 198 *Brighton &*
	The Downs 1:50,000
Accommodation:	Truleigh Hill - Youth Hostel (on route)
	Edburton - Hotel & b&b (1-1½ miles off route)
	Bramber - Hotel (1 mile off route)

This part of the walk is broken into two distinct stages. The first short leg climbs out of Pyecombe, crosses West Hill and drops then to the few barns and cottages of Saddlescombe which is, in true geographical terms, set as a saddle, or pass, in a combe. Ahead rises the scrub and tree-covered Devil's Dyke where the second stage of the walk tackles a confusing route climbing onto the back of the Downs once more. West of Devil's Dyke the way leads on a regular rise and fall of hills, often with distant views blinkered by higher ground to the north. Over the cluttered summit of Truleigh Hill the track takes us down all the way to the Shoreham road, then over the River Adur to meet the end of the Downs Link path near St. Botolph's church.

Refreshment facilities along this part of the route are available at the Devil's Dyke Hotel. In addition there are two drinking water taps; the first by the entrance to Truleigh Hill Youth Hostel, the second a few yards before the bridge over the Adur.

* * *

Cross the A23 by the Plough Inn at Pyecombe and walk along a narrow lane opposite which goes beside some riding stables. When the lane swings to the right, leave it and continue ahead, through a bridle gate and wander uphill beside a hawthorn hedge to a gate near the brow of the hill. Continue through this for a further 200 yards, then take the right-hand track. (The left-hand bridleway goes to Patcham.) At this point you can see the tall buildings of Brighton way off to the left, while if you turn around you'll see the Clayton Windmills on the far hill. Wandering ahead along the track the Devil's Dyke shows itself clearly.

The trail now plunges down a steep grass slope, at the foot of which you go through a bridle gate next to a stile, and down then along an enclosed track, sunken in places, among hedges and trees. This comes to a large farm and a row of cottages at Saddlescombe. (Grid ref: 273115) Walk ahead between farm buildings and the cottages, then

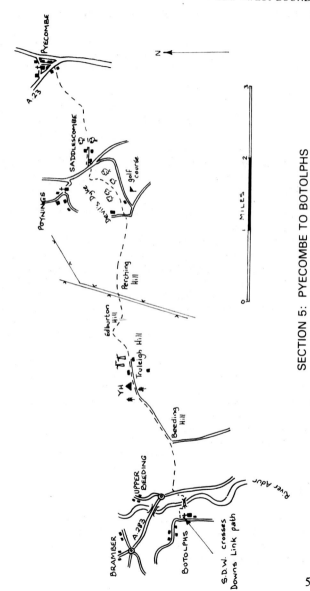

SECTION 5: PYECOMBE TO BOTOLPHS

veer left beyond the farm, pass in front of another cottage and come to a road.

Cross to a broad track clearly seen winding uphill, passing an underground reservoir and coming onto Summer Down. (Cars are frequently parked here which, sadly, means the inevitable litter.) A narrow road runs across Summer Down on your left, linking the road previously crossed at Saddlescombe with another which goes up to the hotel on Devil's Dyke. A number of tracks leading among trees and scrub make the way rather confusing over Summer Down and Devil's Dyke (1), but you must attempt to find a broad flint trail south of the hotel (which can be seen across the combe of the Dyke) and which emerges onto the approach road some 200 yards south of the hotel and opposite a bridle gate. (**Note:** *Should you misjudge the way and find yourself on the road near a golf course - easily done - bear right and follow this road past the clubhouse, then turn right at a T junction to walk up the hotel approach road until you come to the signposted continuing route on the left.*)

From the hotel approach road go through the bridle gate and cross a broad meadow left of the trig point and earth ramparts of the Iron Age hill fort, and make for the far left-hand corner where another gate takes the route along a track with a fence on the left.

The South Downs Way being bridleway as well as a walking route, I had seen several horse riders along the journey from Eastbourne - none actually tackling the route, but out enjoying an hour or so's exercise. But bridleways are also permissible routes for cyclists and I knew one or two keen 'rough-stuff' riders who had tackled various stages of the SDW in the past. Yet coming to the end of the meadow near Devil's Dyke hill fort I was still surprised to meet a lone cyclist on a mountain bike coming towards me. It pleased me no end to see that he appeared every bit as weary as I felt at this point, and I held the gate open for him to ride through. Watching him bump across the meadow, raised uncomfortably above the saddle as he avoided the cowpats, I was immensely relieved to be a mere walker and wandered on feeling strangely comforted.

Heading north-westwards cross Fulking Hill with fine views to north and south, then over Perching Hill towards a row of pylons carrying overhead power lines. Passing beneath the cables there are cross tracks (north to drop into the Weald at Fulking, south through the heartland of the Downs to Southwick and the sea).

Continue straight ahead on a white chalk track sweeping uphill through fields to Edburton Hill. Another crossing bridleway gives the opportunity for walkers to cut down to accommodation in Edburton but the route proper continues onto Truleigh Hill with its cluster of masts and untidy buildings. Freshcombe Lodge and Truleigh Hill Farm come next, then the Youth Hostel standing only a few paces from the track among pine trees. (Grid ref: 220105)

Continue beyond the Youth Hostel, and a few yards after a line of pine trees there is a narrow footpath running parallel with the track on the right. The two merge where the track makes a sharp left-hand bend by a most attractive six-direction finger post erected by the Society of Sussex Downsmen in 1973 to mark its golden jubilee.

Go straight ahead, through a bridle gate and follow a meadowland path heading half-right towards a field gate. On passing through this a fence-enclosed track descends to the A283 a little north of an ugly cement works. The village of Upper Beeding is a short distance away to the right.

Bear left along the road for nearly 150 yards, then cross over to a lay-by to find a gate giving access to an enclosed path. In a few paces you will come to a water tap and some seats. The path swings to the right, crosses a footbridge (specially built for the South Downs Way) over the River Adur, and bears right alongside the river. About 150 yards further on, head to the left on another path beside a ditch. A few moments later you cross the bed of a former railway line which is the path of the Downs Link (2). There is an information board beside the path. Continue ahead for a few more paces and come to a quiet road. (Grid ref: 194093) St. Bololph's church is seen off to the left.

There's nothing here, apart from a quiet Saxon church that glows a soft orange towards sunset, a farm or two and a few cottages. This is the hamlet of Botolphs; no pub, no shops, no overnight accommodation for travellers. For that we must go north to Bramber or Steyning. But Botolphs once was considerably larger, for it had a salt industry - and fishing - until the sea drew back from the valley of the Adur and left the village literally high and dry. In the Middle Ages its fortunes drifted out with the tide, and the odd hummocks in the meadows are all that remain of one-time village houses.

Things Seen On The Way:

1: *Devil's Dyke.* Legend has it that the Devil attempted to carve a dyke through the Downs in order to allow the sea to flood the churches of the Weald. Working at night he shovelled the earth into great mounds, but was disturbed in his fiendish task when he saw an old lady carrying a candle, which he took for the dawn. The earth mounds the Devil was apparently shovelling are the assorted tumuli of the area and the massive Iron Age hill fort on the summit. Devil's Dyke is a popular place with hang-gliding enthusiasts.

2: *The Downs Link.* On this stage at Botolphs the South Downs Way meets the end of the Downs Link, the long-distance footpath which follows the bed of a one-time railway for much of its 33-mile journey from St. Martha's Hill near Guildford in Surrey.

Accommodation:

Truleigh Hill	The Youth Hostel, Tottington Barn, Truleigh Hill, Shoreham-by-Sea, BN4 5FB. Tel: Steyning 813419
Edburton	Tottington Manor Hotel, Edburton, Henfield, BN5 9LJ. Tel: Steyning 815757
	Mrs. O'Brecht, Paythorne Farmhouse, Edburton, Henfield, BN5 9LP. Tel: Poynings 259
	Mrs. Clement, Aburton Farm, Edburton, Henfield, BN5 9LN. Tel: Poynings 388
	Mrs. Turk, Truleigh Cottage, Browns Meadow, Edburton, Henfield, BN5 2LN. Tel: Poynings 245
Bramber	Green Leaves Hotel, Clays Hill, Bramber, Steyning, BN4 3WE. Tel: Steyning 813222

Public Transport:

From *Upper Beeding* buses run to Shoreham-on-Sea.

SECTION 6: **BOTOLPHS TO WASHINGTON (A24)**

Distance:	6½ miles
Map:	O.S. Landranger series; Sheet 198 *Brighton & The Downs* 1:50,000
Accommodation:	Washington - Hotel, b&b (1 mile off route)

Climbing out of the valley of the Adur the route soon leads onto the Downs again with some lovely intimate vistas of knuckled combes and mounded brows. A short stretch of country lane leads across the head of Steyning Bowl, then it's back to bridleway again heading into a broad inner countryside of wood-lined fields over Steyning Round Hill where a large number of Bronze Age cremation urns were discovered in 1949.

Chanctonbury Ring is visited. This crown of beech and sycamore, seen from so many different points on the Downs and from the Weald below, was badly hit by the hurricane of October 1987, but many of the trees survived and it remains a highlight of the walk from Eastbourne to Winchester.

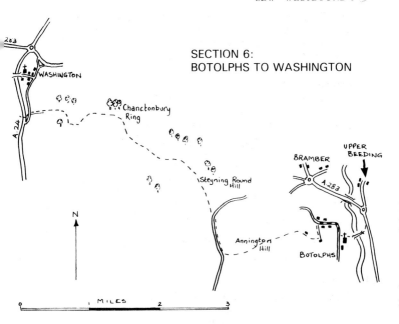

SECTION 6:
BOTOLPHS TO WASHINGTON

(When the South Downs Way went no farther than Buriton, Chanctonbury Ring marked the halfway point.) On this hilltop the lovely clump of trees adorns the site of an Iron Age fort and a Roman temple, while a couple of miles or so away to the south, Cissbury Ring is the largest and most impressive of all the earthworks on the South Downs where remains of a remarkable 200-odd Neolithic flint mines have been found. Cissbury, however, is not on the line of our walk.

Beyond Chanctonbury a shrub-lined track winds down to the dry valley cut by the busy A24 on the outskirts of Washington village.

There are no refreshments available on this stage, but there is a pub in Washington, just off the route, for those in need of a drink or a meal at the end of the walk.

★ ★ ★

The South Downs Way, having crossed the line of the Downs Link at the end of Section 5, comes to a country road in the hamlet of Botolphs. Turn right and wander along it (heading away from the church) for about half a mile and passing one or two farms on the way. Walking uphill the road swings sharply to the right, but the South Downs Way breaks off to the left along a track shaded by trees and signposted to Tinpots Cottage. Shortly before the cottage the track veers to the right climbing onto the back of the Downs. As you gain height there is a tendency to keep peering off to the left where folding hills tuck themselves into Winding Bottom; a most attractive little vale with Coombe Head protecting it to the south. The sea lies not much more than three miles away, but the South Downs are beginning to edge their way inland, and there will not be many more views of its distant glimmer or sheen.

The track leads to Annington Hill where you follow a reasonably straight course along the crest. At the end of a long arable section jumpy with skylarks go through a metal field gate, turn right and descend along the edge of the next field for a short distance until you come to a fenced area known as Bramber Beeches where the West Sussex Federation of Women's Institutes planted a little woodland of beech and pine to mark its diamond jubilee in 1979. Now bear left and continue along the field edge beside a fence towards the distant road. (To the right lies Steyning Bowl, a soft combe flowing north-eastwards to the interesting and historic village of Steyning.)

On reaching the narrow hilltop road turn right and wander along it for about half a mile, then when it veers towards the right and begins to descend, cross over to a gateway on the left and head half-right across the field (in fact, more or less maintaining direction). You will come to cross-tracks and continue straight ahead. (The left-hand track would lead eventually to Cissbury Ring and Findon.) Before long a trig point is seen in the field a little left of the track marking Steyning Round Hill.

The way is clearly marked with finger posts at all path junctions. The route heads north-westwards and the Downs here have been mostly put to wheat. Ahead the crown of Chanctonbury Ring (1) grows in stature, and the track leads directly to it. Just before reaching it, however, you come to more cross-tracks, the left-hand option being the major linking route between Chanctonbury and Cissbury Rings. The route continues and rises across a green meadowland to pass along the left-hand side of the stand of trees. (Grid ref: 139120)

I'd looked forward to greeting the hilltop grove of beeches for some time, but feared what I might find after the ravages of the great storm. From afar Chanctonbury has seemed to have survived. I'd looked up from the depths of the Weald and gazed to it from prominent positions along the eastern Downs, and all had appeared well. But as I walked across the meadow now, so the grey light of an overcast day shone through and I could see the leaning trunks, the huge upturned discs of earth, the exposed and ruptured root systems, and my heart fell. For two hundred years these trees had impressed themselves on the Sussex landscape, but a tremendous, horrendous, unexpected gale in the early hours of October 16th 1987 effectively altered that landscape. From close inspection it looked as though a good 50% of the trees were down. Many were trapped at drunken angles, others lay horizontal, yet more were torn and twisted, their limbs hanging sadly with exposed subcutaneous tissue glimmering a ghostly white in the gloom. It was a pitiful sight, but I have great faith in the determination of man to restore such places, and have no doubt that by the time this guide is published the remnants of the storm will have been cleared away and replacement beeches planted. There will come a new tomorrow, and Chanctonbury's Ring of trees will continue to be a highlight and a symbol of the glorious Sussex Downs.

Walk along the southern side of the trees heading due west. You will pass a trig point and then, veering a little leftwards, go through a bridle gate beside a cattle-grid with a restored dew pond on the right, and continue ahead along the tree and shrub-lined track. Very soon you will come to a major junction of tracks where you turn right for the winding descent on rough flints to the A24 a little south of Washington. (Grid ref: 120120)

Note: *For refreshment or accommodation in Washington, do not cross the A24, but instead bear right along the old road before it. This leads directly to the village.*

Things Seen On The Way:

1: *Chanctonbury Ring.* Planted in 1760 by Charles Goring of Wiston House, below to the north-east, the grove of beech and sycamore was especially set to delight the eye. And it certain does just that. An Iron Age fort of about four acres forms the base of the Ring, and in the heart of it the Romans built a temple during the 3rd or 4th century. Before the hurricane ripped through there was a distinctive yet indescribable atmosphere to be experienced within the Ring; a halo of enchantment that no doubt will return once the sad remains of the storm have been cleared. Magnificent views may be had from the edge of the trees.

Accommodation:

Washington   Washington Towers Hotel, London Road,
Washington, Pulborough, RH20 4AT.
Tel: Ashington 892869 *(Camping allowed)*
Mr. & Mrs. Langley, Rock Windmill, The Hollow,
Washington, Pulborough, RH20 3DA.
Tel: Ashington 892941
Mrs. Ward, Brook House, Washington,
Pulborough, RH20 4AL, Tel: Ashington 892142

Public Transport:

Washington has bus links with Worthing (rail to Brighton) Storrington
and Pulborough, and Horsham (not Sundays).

SECTION 7:   **WASHINGTON TO AMBERLEY STATION
(Arun Valley)**

Distance:	6½ miles
Maps:	O.S. Landranger series; Sheets 198 *Brighton & The Downs* and 197 *Chichester & The Downs* 1:50,000
Accommodation:	Amberley - b&b
	Houghton - b&b (½ mile ahead on Section 8)
	Warningcamp - Youth Hostel (Arundel) (3 miles off route)

Between the deep cut of the A24 and the twisting river valley of the Arun, the Downs present a broad-topped escarpment, tufted here and there with trees, fields sown with wheat, barley or rape. In places the long-distance walker is rewarded with views into the depths of the Weald; sometimes over villages, sometimes over lonely farms and later, over the glint and glimmer of the Arun drawing itself uncomfortably through the low country to the north. Down there, too, seen best from Rackham Banks, are the water meadows of Amberley Wild Brooks; marshlands drained by dykes and ditches, a criss-cross of watercourses picked out by the sun. Beyond the marshes and Arun's valley the wall of the Downs slopes onward in an enticing curve. It's another stage without habitation, though there are one or two isolated barns, and at Chantry Hill and Springhead Hill narrow lanes come onto the lip of the Downs from Storrington, whose village houses are tucked against the northern slopes. Cattle graze in large open meadows.

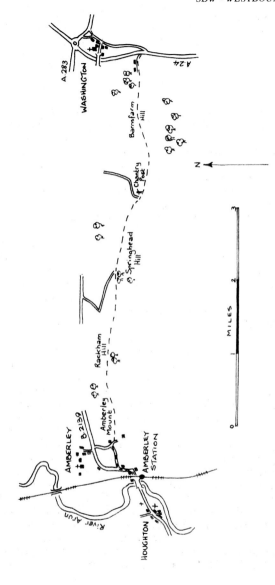

SECTION 7: WASHINGTON TO AMBERLEY STATION

There are hares and peewits and big skies conjuring Turner canvases on wild-weather days.

Within a short distance of the start there is a water tap. Beyond, nothing until you reach the Bridge Inn near Amberley Station.

* * *

Cross the dual carriageway of the A24 with great care and enter Glaseby Road opposite. (**Note:** *Should traffic be too horrendous to face, do not cross here, but bear right along the old road and walk into Washington village. Then bear left on the approach to the parish church, cross the bridge over A24 and immediately turn left along a footpath which brings you in half a mile to Glaseby Lane. Turn right on the SDW.)*

Glaseby Lane winds uphill and about 200 yards from the main road you will pass a drinking tap on the left. The surfaced lane ends and becomes a flint track climbing Highden Hill. As the initial shading trees recede so the countryside opens out again. A couple of fields away to the left there stretches a large woodland. Wandering through broad fields the way leads onto the crest of Barnsfarm Hill where you meet another track coming from the right (an alternative route from Washington). The way continues towards a Dutch barn and, following a fence across the grasslands of Sullington Hill, eventually reaches a car parking area on Chantry Hill overlooking Storrington. (Grid ref: 087119) This is a noted local viewpoint with one or two seats placed by the Chantry Post. (Unfortunately this, like the Keymer Post near Ditchling Beacon on Section 4, is subjected to mindless vandalism.)

I had already been walking for several hours when I arrived at the Chantry Post, so sat with my back against it to eat my sandwiches. Almost immediately the heavy clouds overhanging Storrington swung away to the west, rose up the hillside and perched sullenly on Springhead Hill to block my advance. The air turned cool, a breeze huffed across the Downs and suddenly lightning streaked the sky. Thunder roared and the ground shook. There was nowhere to hide. No shelter from the rain that came racing in great rods from the west, so I put my sandwiches away, pulled on waterproofs and headed into the eye of the storm. A magical pathway then led between the shafts of lightning (fence posts of fire), though I saw little of the countryside to the right or left, blinkered as I was by the visor of my cagoule. Twenty minutes later the worst was over and I resumed my lunch among the puddles of a dripping spinney.

With the Chantry Post to your right continue straight ahead along a clear flint track which gently crosses a line of minor hills in a north-westerly direction. In places (so it is claimed) a view opens to the left to show the sea and the edge of the Isle of Wight far off. On meeting the head of another small lane on Springhead Hill the route veers slightly left to head west. There are hedges and clumps of trees, much arable farmland, and then passing through a little woodland at last the track gives way to soft grass under foot. A relief after the sharp flints.

All around Rackham Hill there are tumuli. To the south, a mile or so away and reached by a track known as the Lepers Way, is the site of a Bronze Age barrow (The Burgh), while ahead, alongside the route over Amberley Mount, there are lynchets which an archaeological survey revealed as a system of twenty fields, some of which had been terraced two and a half thousand years ago.

Along the grassy track by Rackham Banks you gain those splendid views into the Weald and ahead, across the Arun's gap, to the wooded slopes of the South Downs curving far away into the distance, luring you on. It is a lovely stretch of walk, easy underfoot, easy on the eye, and soon the route leads to a gate with the large conglomeration of barns and outbuildings of Downs Farm seen below. Go through the gate and descend the slope to pass well to the right of the farm. An enclosed path then leads to a road where you bear right for about 80 yards, then on coming to a junction head left along High Titton Lane. (Grid ref: 034125)

Note: *For those planning to stay overnight in Amberley, the shortest route is to ignore the turning into High Titton Lane and continue instead along the narrow road which slopes down to meet the B2139 at a small crossroads. Cross directly ahead into the village.*

High Titton Lane in fact leads between two deep chalk quarries (that on the right is mostly hidden by bushes and trees) and brings you to the B2139 Storrington to Houghton road. Turn left along the road. There is soon a safe footpath to follow along the right-hand side. This winds down to Amberley Station, with the Bridge Inn just beyond it on the left. (By the station is Amberley Chalk Pits Museum.)

Note: *There is a water tap outside the pub; also refreshments available in a tea-shop near the bridge over the Arun. Walkers planning to stay overnight at Arundel Youth Hostel could catch a train here for Arundel - the next station down the line - and walk from there one mile north-east. Alternatively, walk along the lane beside the Bridge Inn as far as North Stoke, then by a combination of footpath and lane to Warningcamp.*

Accommodation:

Amberley   Mrs. Clyde, Leith House, East Street, Amberley, Arundel, BN18 9NP. Tel: Bury 895

Mrs. Gilbert, Wisteria Cottage, East Street, Amberley, Arundel. Tel: Bury 340

Houghton Mrs. Caldwell, Green Bottle, South Lane, Houghton, Arundel, BN18 9LN. Tel: Bury 854

Warningcamp Arundel Youth Hostel, Warningcamp, Arundel, BN18 9QY. Tel: Arundel 882204

Public Transport:
From *Amberley* trains run to Arundel and Littlehampton, Pulborough and Horsham.

SECTION 8: **AMBERLEY STATION TO COCKING**

Distance: 11 miles
Map: O.S. Landranger series; Sheet 197 *Chichester & The Downs* 1:50,000
Accommodation: Cocking - b&b

Given private transport arrangements this lengthy stage could be broken after about six miles at the crossing of A285, some five miles or so south of Petworth. Otherwise it will be necessary to complete the walk as far as Cocking.

After a short road section to Houghton the route heads away from traffic to climb onto the Downs once more, passing woods and entering a hidden landscape of blending hill and vale, then out onto open skies on Bignor Hill. Soon after this the South Downs Way crosses the route of the Roman Stane Street; an historic area, not just from the Roman era, but long before.

Burton Down gives way to more arable land, but on the stage west of the A285 there is much woodland and views are severely restricted for several miles. Strips of farmland break up the extensive woods, and it is with some relief that Manorfarm Down opens a vista above the friendly little village of Cocking; a village with an attractive heart and with its welcome prospects of refreshment and lodging.

Fill water bottles at the start of this stage for there are no further opportunities for refreshment until Cocking is reached.

* * *

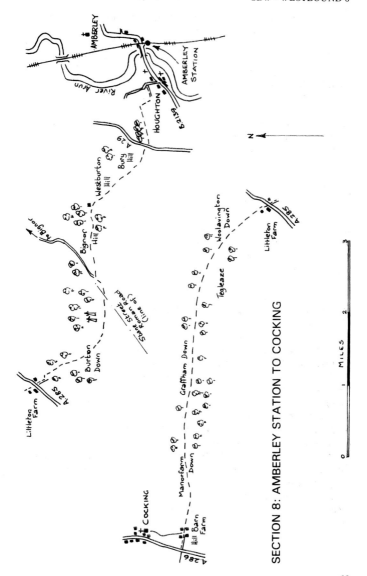

SECTION 8: AMBERLEY STATION TO COCKING

Cross the River Arun (1) and wander ahead along the road into Houghton village, (2) then after passing the Parish church (on the left) take the first turning on the right; a country lane with the charming thatched roofed 'Old Farm' at its entrance. The lane drops and winds out of the village, and about 250 yards along it a track breaks away to the left between fields. Walk along this as it climbs the hillside to Coombe Wood and, shortly after, comes onto the Bury-Arundel road. (Grid ref: 003118) Bear right for 100 yards, then leave the road to follow a chalk track heading left towards Houghton Forest. Beside the forest the way bears right, soon leaving the edge of the trees, and cuts through open fields on Bury Hill. *('To this green hill a something dream-like clings...'* said Galsworthy in his poem, 'Bury Hill'.)

Before long the track becomes enclosed by fences and there are cowslips in the grassy banks along Westburton Hill. Then you slope down to some black barns caught in a hollow, and just beyond them come to a junction of tracks. Bear left, then straight away turn right to climb uphill alongside hedges, over cross-tracks and continue ahead beside a fence which leads to Bignor Hill. *(To the north, at the foot of the Downs, lie the ruins of Bignor Roman Villa, centre of a 2,000 acre estate. The mosaics preserved at the villa are truly magnificent and well worth a visit.)*

At a bridle gate a little east of Bignor Hill you arrive at Toby's Stone - a mounting-block memorial to one-time secretary to the Cowdray Hounds, Toby Wentworth-Fitzwilliam.

The way continues, now heading a little south of west, and comes to a car parking area almost on the line of the Roman road of Stane Street (3). An interesting finger post here gives directions to Noviomagus, Bignor and Londinium. Passing this post on your left continue ahead towards a pair of aerials. About 200 yards from the post bear left along Stane Street, then turn right at the first junction among some scrub. Now alongside a field with the aerial masts off to your right, maintain direction until another junction of paths. Continue ahead, passing a few yew trees on Burton Down and now heading north-westward, once more walking across arable land before descending through woods on a clear track which leads to the A285 at Littleton Farm. (Grid ref: 951144)

Coming down the track in the mid-afternoon birds were mostly speechless, but there were numerous wild flowers clustered at the base of the trees and along the banks to brighten the way. Small flies danced as though riding gossamer yo-yos in misted beams of sunlight that chequered the track around me, and I wandered down on stepping stones of shadow.

Cross the road and take the track opposite which goes to the right of

Toby's Stone on Bignor Hill

the farm between grassy banks and trees. On coming to cross-tracks go into the field ahead (to the right of a track climbing uphill) and cross uphill through the field, veering slightly to the right in order to find another bridle gate in a mid-field fence. Continue ahead to the upper edge of the top field. *(My heart went into my mouth as a partridge leapt out of the young corn beside me, and when I recovered my shock and looked around, there were the pleading eyes of the hen bird gazing pitifully at me from her maternal egg-protecting squat. The cock had raced away to distract my attention from the nest, leaving the hen bravely sitting out the danger. 'You're safe from me, old girl,' I told her. Then scolded her nesting site. 'Bloody daft place to lay your eggs though. The path'll be crawling with ramblers 'ere long.' Leaving her in peace I almost detected her sigh of relief.)* At the head of the field wander ahead on a broad track leading through woodland.

There now follows a long section beside Tegleaze Woods and over Woolavington Down. (Solitary walkers may catch sight of deer along this section, and indeed, almost anywhere between here and Cocking.) Emerging from the first patch of woods walk along a clear track heading north-west with the woods on your left. Ignoring alternative signposted paths, stay with the main track for about a mile, then it leads through scrub and woods for a further mile or so over Graffham

Down. This track is sometimes soft and muddy and in places there is little alternative but to squelch through where the trees and bushes reduce the margins. There are other tracks cutting away here and there, but the South Downs Way is clearly defined.

Shortly after coming to a section of conifers on the right, the Heyshott Down archaeological site is seen also on the right. The track bears left, then right again with a large field spreading ahead. Walk along the left-hand edge of the field, in the middle of which you will see a trig point and a timber-built hunting platform.

Pass through a gate at the far end of the field and continue ahead, still beside woods for a while. The flint track then descends through a much more open countryside on Manorfarm Down and comes to Hill Barn Farm.

Note: *On the left, by the entrance to a sawmill, there is a drinking water tap.*

Note also: *For those planning to stay overnight in Cocking, bear right through the farm on a track which leads down to the village and brings you out by the lovely church.*

Continue ahead for the main South Downs Way route and you will shortly come to the A286 a little south of Cocking.

Cocking village is an attractive place. A small village astride the A286, it remains remarkably untouched by the busy road. A number of houses in and around the village form part of the Cowdray Estate, and the yellow painted window frames are an indication of this. There was a settlement here long before the Norman Conquest, and the Domesday Book records '... a Church, 6 serfs and 5 mills yielding 37 shillings and sixpence.' The church stands on the eastern edge of the village with fields around it and Manor Farm sharing its churchyard wall. Below it runs a clear stream in a delightful setting. Cocking has two pubs, Post Office Stores and b&b accommodation.

Things Seen On The Way:

1: *River Arun.* Of the four Sussex rivers that breach the South Downs, the Arun is the longest. During the Napoleonic Wars a canal was built to join the Arun with the Thames via the River Wey. A wharf stood on the river then, near Houghton bridge, and chalk barges traded along the navigation. The canal was closed in 1868, but restoration work has taken place on short sections of it in recent years. (It may be of interest to note that the Downs Link follows part of the old canal in its northern section, and the Wey-South Path attempts to accompany it all the way from Guildford to Amberley. Route guide: *The Wey-South Path* by Aeneas Mackintosh, available from the Wey &

Arun Canal Trust Ltd.) Today the River Arun has a cheery aspect near the bridge. It's tidal, a good place for water fowl and small boats.

: *Houghton* stands a little above the Arun. There are several interesting buildings, one of which, the George and Dragon, is where the young Charles II supposedly stopped for refreshment in October 1651 during his flight to France following defeat in the Battle of Worcester.

: *Stane Street* is a Saxon name for a Roman road originally built for both military and economic purposes to link Chichester (Noviomagus) with London (Londinium). This remarkable piece of engineering had to cross not only the South and North Downs, but also the greensand range and the almost inpenetrable Wealden forest. It achieved the 56 mile route in three die-straight lines, including a passage through the 2,000 acre estate attached to the Roman Villa at Bignor, which is found below the Downs a short distance away from the point at which the South Downs Way crosses.

Accommodation:

Cocking	J.Cooper, The Old Rectory, Bell Lane, Cocking, Midhurst, GU29 0HU. Tel: Midhurst 4239
	Mrs. Marks, Manor Farm, Cocking, Midhurst *(Also camping)* Tel: Midhurst 2784
	Mrs. Wooldridge, Alpenrose, Cocking, Midhurst, GU29 0HN. Tel: Midhurst 3298
	Mrs. Caldwell, Downsfold, Bell Lane, Cocking, Midhurst, GU29 0HU. Tel: Midhurst 4376
	Mrs. Johnston, Keeper's Cottage, Cocking, Midhurst. Tel: Midhurst 2762
	Mrs. Daynes-Winter, Chalk Way Cottage, Cocking, Midhurst. Tel: Midhurst 4202

Public Transport:
Buses lead from *Cocking* to Midhurst, Singleton and Chichester.

SECTION 9:   COCKING TO SOUTH HARTING

Distance:	7½ miles
Map:	O.S. Landranger series; Sheet 197 *Chichester & The Downs* 1:50,000

Accommodation: South Harting - b&b

A very fine walk, this is, full of variety and interest. There are sections where the views are extensive, and others where woodland draws a secluded landscape. There are remarkably isolated farms tucked away from the world just off the path, practically no other habitation and no village of any size at all for many a long mile. Once again the route takes you along the northern edge of the escarpment, but gazing south you may catch a glimpse of the spire of Chichester Cathedral framed in a tree-crowded panorama. In the woods encroaching on the trail it is possible you might catch sight of deer. Certainly there will be numerous birds to serenade the day, and wild flowers in plenty.

An easy track leads onto Cocking Down, then to Linch Down, broad and open. Monkton Down leads to Philliswood, and emerging from the light glades of these woods a delightful countryside is revealed. On the approach to Beacon Hill one rejoices in marvellous vistas, and over Harting Down you gaze north over plunging slopes of green to tiny communities lost in the shadows of the Downs. Rarely will you walk this last downland brow alone, for there's a car park nearby and a road that leads from Petersfield. A path running adjacent to the B2146 drops down for nearly a mile to South Harting, while the continuing route avoids the village and goes on towards Hampshire and the former end to the South Downs Way at Buriton.

Yet again this stage is entirely without any hope of refreshment, so set out for the day suitably provisioned. (The pub in South Harting serves meals.)

*   *   *

The South Downs Way reaches the A286 from Hillbarn Lane a little south of Cocking village. Cross the road and continue ahead in the same direction along Middlefield Lane to pass a farm with yellow windows, and wander up the track towards Cocking Down. The white chalk track is enclosed at first by hedges, but on the crest of the Downs bare fences replace the ever-interesting hedgerows, while off to the left stretch extensive woodlands. Now and again hides can be seen in them, as well as in one or two fields. (There are many deer in these woods and they cause considerable damage to crops - often by sleeping in small herds in the cornfields, thus crushing the crop and making harvest difficult.)

For three miles the track maintains a steady direction across Cocking Down, Linch Down (with its trig point in the middle of a field to the right) and Didling Hill. On a clear day not only is Chiches

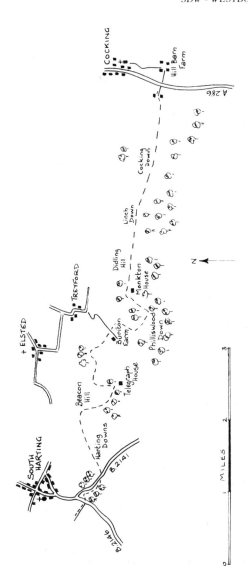

SECTION 9: COCKING TO SOUTH HARTING

ter Cathedral spire seen across the intervening woods, but also the Solent and the Isle of Wight beyond. Mostly this crown of hills has been turned to arable farming, but there are grasslands on Didling Hill white with sheep; fenced meadows that need no shepherd on watch.

Then the enclosed track is absorbed by a tunnel of trees and scrub with a high fence on the left containing the secluded, virtually unseen, Monkton House. In its grounds there are peacocks screeching. *(One had somehow escaped the lofty barrier and it ran ahead of me along the track, dragging its exotic feathers behind, reminding me of a bride opting for extravagant fashion rather than a tradition of white. Now and then it stopped to check if I were still following, then took off once more. Stupid bird, I feared I might chase it all the way to Winchester.)*

Now the track swings to the left and enters the woods of Philliswood Down. Lovely mature trees; beech and oak and birch, many of which have been damaged in the hurricane. On the right as you enter these woods, five successive tumuli, or burial mounds, have been cleared of scrub and excavated. These, known as the Devil's Jumps, date from the Bronze Age (about 3,500 years ago).

As you wander through the woods enjoying birdsong, the multi-shades of green in the leaves and on the trunks of the beeches and in the ground cover of sunlit glades, keep alert for the cross-tracks where the South Downs Way breaks away sharply to the right. Now follow a fence on the left as you wander north-westwards, soon to leave the woods behind while ahead views open to include both wood and downland, with the little villages of Treyford and Elsted in the distance. Across to the left the shape of Telegraph House (1) may be seen above the trees on the southern slopes of Beacon Hill.

Continue down the slope on a track that becomes a sunken one in places, and with cowslips painting the banks yellow in spring. Then you reach a narrow farm track (Grid ref: 821178) and see off to the left Buriton Farm squatting shyly in a dip of folding hills. *(By following this track to the right you would escape the embrace of the Downs and come to the hamlet of Treyford. Charming as it might be, and inviting as many of these downland tracks are as they wind into a no-man's land of beauty, this is not on the route of the SDW.)* Bear left for a few paces, then head to the right, through a bridle gate and onto an enclosed track heading again towards the north-west. You will come to the edge of a spinney which you skirt along its left-hand edge, then follow along the bottom edge of a field, over a crossing track (the right-hand trail goes to Elsted) and veering leftwards climb the slope ahead on a scrub-and-thorn-lively margin between fields. This is Pen Hill, and from its crest

*Chalk tracks on the Downs: Pen Hill, looking
towards Beacon Hill*

there is a wonderful panorama to be had.

*Warm now, I stripped off my shirt and lay in the grass gazing into a
hazy blue vault where half a dozen skylarks trilled with an enthusiasm
impossible to check. Turning to the east my eye caught the sweeping Downs
brunched with spring colours in the trees and shrubs on the northern slopes.
To the west Beacon Hill, site of an Iron Age hill fort of forty acres, was
scarred with two distinct white tracks across which shadowy four-legged
figures loped to and fro. Far-off views were distorted, but that did not
matter. Nearer to hand were flowers in the field margins and blossom
among the blackthorn. I saw a rabbit break cover and nervously make a
stuttering run across the bay below. Ants pioneered a new route up the face
of an upturned slice of flint. A pheasant crackled. A cuckoo called. Sheep
in valley meadows sent messages in the breeze. Unused to such busy peace,
city folk might call this silence. It was not. In the calm hush of morning
were countless sounds of life - but nothing at all with an engine. All was just
as it should be.*

Looking at Beacon Hill to the west note that it is the left-hand chalk
track that should be taken (although the right-hand option makes a
short cut over the summit of the hill and rejoins the SDW proper at
Bramshott Bottom, thus saving about three quarters of a mile).

Descend steeply to the saddle between Pen Hill and Beacon Hill, then fork left to traverse round the slopes above the combe known as Millpond Bottom. The way takes you along the edge of a large field and comes to trees, scrub and gorse near the entrance to Telegraph House. At a crossing track a few paces later head sharply to the right along a scrub-lined track with a variety of plants growing beside it. This leads along Bramshott Bottom, a grassy vale, and comes to cross-tracks where you turn left to climb onto Harting Downs - a popular excursion for motorists who park on the western side.

The views from the springy turf crown of downland are lovely and considerable in extent. A number of little villages may be seen below, pre-eminent being South Harting with a green copper broach spire to its church. (There's a South Harting, East Harting and West Harting. Whatever happened to North Harting?)

Continue across Harting Down to reach the car park, then walk along its right-hand side to the B2141 road, cross over and take the track beyond as it delves among fine mature beech, oak and chestnut trees, and runs parallel with the road, steadily losing height. This very pleasant stretch is known as The Bosom.

On coming to another road (the B2146) cross over to find the continuing track a little to the right, (Grid ref: 783185) and here leave the South Downs Way by breaking away to the right on a footpath leading down to South Harting.

South Harting is a compact little village with a fine 14th century church dedicated to St. Mary and St. Gabriel. Shortly before he died Anthony Trollope lived here. Refreshments, including meals are available at the White Hart Inn.

Things Seen On The Way:

1: *Telegraph House:* Hidden at the end of a long drive on the southern slopes of Beacon Hill, Telegraph House was built by Earl Russell at the turn of the century on the site of one of the Admiralty's Portsmouth to London telegraph stations. Later, Earl Russell's brother, the philosopher Bertrand Russell, turned it into a (short-lived) school.

Accommodation:

South Harting: Mrs. Wroe, Foxcombe House, South Harting, Petersfield, GU31 5PL. Tel: Harting 357

Public Transport:

South Harting is served with buses to Midhurst and Petersfield (not Sundays).

SECTION 10: **SOUTH HARTING TO BURITON**
(Queen Elizabeth Forest)

Distance:	3½ miles
Map:	O.S. Landranger series; Sheet 197 *Chichester &* *The Downs* 1:50,000
Accommodation.	Buriton - b&b

This very short stage marks the original completion of the South Downs Way and takes the route out of Sussex and into Hampshire. It is also a stage which notes a change in landscape, for gone - temporarily - are the rolling Downs and in their place comes a typical southern countryside of seemingly low farmland with woods and hedgerows and winding lanes. But it is no less interesting for that. There are plenty of flowers in the hedgerows and field margins, and there's no shortage of wildlife either. There will be jackdaws, no doubt, circling above the woods, and rabbits nose-twitching along the track. It is an easy stage which brings a new dimension to the walk.

From the point at which Section 9 broke from the waymarked route to visit South Harting, a two-mile hedge-lined track leads over farmland with long views into the Weald, and reaches a farm on the county boundary. A quiet country lane takes over, then back to rutted track again at Coulters Dean Farm. At the western end of this track another lane continues among woods to the edge of the pretty village of Buriton. Ahead stretches Queen Elizabeth Forest ready to be tackled at the start of the next stage.

Although there are no refreshment facilities along the route, Buriton has pubs serving food.

* * *

From the point beside the B2146 road at which the previous section finished (Grid ref: 783185), follow the clear hedge-lined track which leads north-westwards with views off to the right. This track is known as Forty Acre Lane and it leads for nearly a mile across a gentle farmland to a crossing metalled lane by a handful of cottages. (At the end of the lane on the left is Foxwood Farm tucked against a large woodland.) Cross over and continue in the same direction ahead on the second half of Forty Acre Lane. Near the end of this, just before Sunwood Farm, you will cross out of Sussex. The track brings you onto a quiet country road by Sunwood Farm where you turn left. In a few yards the road swings to the right and winds easily up a gentle

73

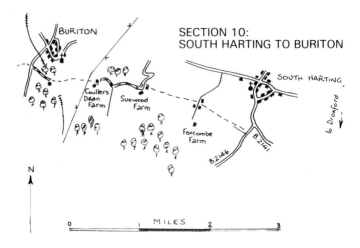

slope beside a row of lovely copper beeches.

These are not the Downs you've grown used to. Their slopes are ploughed and sown and there are no far views, no distant grasslands mottled with sheep. The character of the land has changed in a subtle way, but only temporarily, for you'll return to the recognisable texture of the South Downs 'ere long. For now wander the lane with eyes and ears alert to catch the pulse of life that is the very heartbeat of this southern county.

The road comes to a minor junction where you branch right. (To the left is the entrance to Ditcham Park School.) Now wandering through Cockshott Wood the road winds on, losing height in green leaf-shade. Ignoring a tempting sign on the right which indicates a cart track to Buriton, follow the road as it swings left and right and comes to Coulters Dean Farm, sheltering in a lonely hollow. A rutted track leads on now, climbing uphill to pass beneath overhead power cables, and you continue ahead beside a hedge on the left and with a fence on the right (the track is liable to be muddy after rain) and eventually come to Dean Barn. A pair of cottages here stand among neat gardens on the edge of more woodlands.

The track gives way to a metalled lane once more and soon reaches a T junction with a car parking area opposite and the extensive Queen Elizabeth Forest rising on the far side. Turn right on the road and wander north for about half a mile to reach Buriton.

With its duckpond by the church, this small village is an attractive huddle of cottages that appear (externally at least) to have resisted the excesses of modernisation. In the Elizabethan Manor House behind the parish church once lived Edward Gibbon, the historian. For its size, Buriton has a laudable number of accommodation addresses.

Accommodation:
Buriton   Mrs. Beeson, The Old Hop Kiln, Bones Lane, Buriton, Petersfield, GU31 5SE. Tel: Petersfield 66822
Mrs. Bushell, Toads Alley, South Lane, Buriton, Petersfield, GU31 5RU. Tel: Petersfield 63880
Mrs. Bray, Nursted Farm, Buriton, Petersfield, GU31 5RW. Tel: Petersfield 64278
Mrs. Moss, Pillmead House, North Lane, Buriton, Petersfield, GU31 5RS. Tel: Petersfield 66795

Public Transport:
Buriton is served by buses leading to Petersfield and Portsmouth (not Sundays).

SECTION 11:   **BURITON TO EXTON (A32)**

Distance:	12½ miles
Maps:	O.S. Landranger series; Sheets 197 *Chichester & The Downs* and 185 *Winchester & Basingstoke Area* 1:50,000
Accommodation:	None on route, but at - Droxford - Motel (2 miles off route) West Meon - Guest-house & b&b (2½ miles off route)

A constantly varied walk, this stage brings the SDW back to downland once more. There are grassy paths, broad tracks and country lanes. There are stretches of dark forest with the possibility of sighting deer, hilltops with vast panoramas spread before you, tree-and-scrub-lined alleyways, open fields and rolling meadows. There is the modern traffic horror of the A3 (mercifully avoided by a subway) and a remarkable demonstration site of Iron Age agriculture. Butser Hill is the highest point, not just of Hampshire, but of the length of the South Downs. You pass between the buildings of HMS Mercury - an incongruous name to be found so far inland with neither sea nor ship in sight - and after crossing the ancient crown of Old Winchester Hill, the route follows a delightful and rare chalk stream to the banks of the River Meon. All in all, this is a most interesting and enjoyable stage.

For those with private means of transport it would be possible to arrange to break the walk at the road junction near HMS Mercury. Although a little over twelve miles is not much for a day's walking, there's a lot of height gain and loss to contend with.

The only refreshment facilities will be found about two miles from the start, at the Queen Elizabeth Country Park Centre.

★ ★ ★

Walk across the car parking area on the western side of the road which leads to Buriton (Grid ref: 734198), and through the bridle gate giving access to the Forestry Commission owned Queen Elizabeth Forest. A broad track leads uphill along the left-hand edge of the forest where beech, pine and cedar mingle happily to form a dark-shadow umbrella. Over the brow of the hill ignore the first track cutting back to the right and proceed ahead until the main track forks. Take the right branch and wander easily downhill in the forest proper now (keeping a lookout for deer) to find a picnic and barbecue area in Gravelhill Bottom. Continue through this to reach a small car park at Benham's Bushes.

All was peaceful along the forest track. Few birds were singing, except far off, and my boots made little sound. I'd been watching and listening for deer when suddenly I became aware of eyes upon me, and turning to the right-hand slope saw a pair of deer gazing in my direction. No body markings could be seen, only heads to one side of a tree, rumps to the other. They watched me and I watched them, but their interest was less intense than mine, once they'd established my lack of threat, and growing bored with the view they soundlessly vanished into the deep security of the forest.

At Benham's Bushes you come to a narrow metalled road where you turn left and wander out of the forest. (There is a bridleway running parallel with the road on its left.) As you exit the forest there are various small grassy areas and a number of laid-out paths. Follow a signposted path on the right leading to the Park Centre.

This is the Queen Elizabeth Country Park and the Centre, with its interpretive displays, public toilets and café, is well worth visiting. It is open daily from 10.00-18.00 between March and October.

Continue beyond the Park Centre on a clear path signposted to

SECTION 11: BURITON TO EXTON

Butser Hill Ancient Farm (1). The path goes beneath the traffic roar of the A3 London to Portsmouth road and reaches the entrance to the farm demonstration site. Bear right and walk alongside the fence enclosing the Ancient Farm, go down a slope and through bridle gates into a lovely extensive grassland. Ahead rises 888 foot Butser Hill (2) topped by a huge telecommunications mast. Dark strips of yew finger from the crest of the hill in direct contrast to the softer green of the grass. Walk ahead up the steep slope of flower-starred downland making more or less towards the mast crown, and near the head of the slope go through a bridle gate and (unless you wish to visit the vantage point near the mast) bear leftwards along the line of fence to find a grass track leading to another bridle gate by the entrance to a car park.

Head to the left along the narrow road - a quiet lane running along the crest of the Downs - and ignore the first junction where another road cuts away to the right bound for East Meon. Continue ahead for a further third of a mile to a second junction of roads where you go to the right along a lane marked *'Unsuitable for Motor Vehicles'*. Passing Homelands Farm the surfaced road becomes a track (a true green lane), goes beneath a line of overhead power cables and continues in almost a straight line for more than a mile, crossing as it does Tegdown Hill and Hyden Hill alongside the oaks and beeches of Hyden Wood.

A soft green shade dappled the path. Newly-unfurled beech leaves were silken to the touch, and with the afternoon light shining through them it was possible to see the outline fuzz of hairs and the rich tracery of veins within. Softly they danced up and down in the two o'clock gasp of air so that the route ahead was seen as through an ever-opening and closing Venetian blind of shadow.

The track leads to a junction of minor roads (Grid ref: 683189) a little east of HMS Mercury. The road north goes to East Meon, south to Clanfield and Horndean. The SDW route crosses straight ahead and within a few paces comes to another junction by the entrance to HMS Mercury, the Naval School of Maritime Operations, Communications and Navigation. Bear right along the road which skirts it. Soon Naval buildings are on either side of the public road (but still no ships!). Continue on the road until at the western end of the inshore establishment, just before you come to a sports field, the road veers left and a tarred road cuts off to the right (signposted to Property Services Agency, amongst others). Walk along the right-hand road-way, now with the sports field on your left, and with the masts of Wether Down directly ahead. The surfaced road becomes a track and leads directly past the radio masts and the site of a long barrow.

Butser Hill Ancient Farm demonstration site

It is good to be away from buildings and a hard surfaced road, and on the Downs once more. Views open up towards the north and the track is confined by a fence and hedges and then becomes a sunken trail alive with rabbits as it drops towards Coombe Cross. Coombe Cross is little more than a couple of cottages on a forgotten road, and the route crosses over and continues straight ahead towards the rise of Henwood Down. About 200 yards from the road the track veers right and leads among scrub and trees that form something of a tunnel. Then, about a third of a mile later at a crossing bridle path, bear left and go through a metal field gate. A grass track heads along the right-hand side of a field and onto a concrete farm road which you follow to its end.

A big open country spreads out. The fields are gold with rape, green or yellow with corn, soft with meadows in which Friesian cattle graze. Downs are rolled out as if for inspection. Henwood Down stands again to the north, the wooded rise of Old Winchester Hill is off in the west and knowing the route leads across it, it seems odd that you must now head away from it to the north. (Those who would walk from A to B by the shortest route should have been with Caesar's troops and forget all about modern long-distance footpaths!)

Bear right along the lane at the end of the concrete farm road, passing cottages and barns, and walk as far as the entrance (on the left) of Whitewool Farm. Go down the farm drive and skirt the handsome half-thatched outbuildings, then veer right on another concrete farm road that soon deteriorates to a rutted track climbing diagonally to the right up the slopes of Whitewool Hanger. (Flowers along the banks and broadening views back into the valley.) On coming to the head of the slope the track emerges onto a narrow lane by a junction of roads. (Those who plan an overnight at West Meon could cut short their journey here by following the road to the right, but they'd miss some of the best parts of this stage of the walk.)

Turn left and follow the lane for about a third of a mile until you reach a small lay-by on the right-hand side of the road. Go through a wooden barrier into Old Winchester Hill National Nature Reserve, then immediately bear left and walk a few yards parallel with the road before veering to the right onto the open downland where you gaze across a hollow to the hill fort summit of Old Winchester Hill (3), and out to a lengthy view of Hampshire's lowlands in the north. It is a popular and most attractive scene.

Wander across the short downland grass heading south (parallel with the road) until you reach a crossing flint track. Bear right and follow this for something like 400 yards (a fence on the left, yew trees

Right: Ditchling Beacon

SUSSEX TRUST
FOR NATURE CONSERVATION

NATURE RESERVE

The Seven Sisters seen from Birling Gap

and scrub on the right) until you reach the entrance to the Iron Age hill fort site. Go through the gate and wander ahead through the centre of this most striking and evident of ancient sites where history is clearly laid out beneath your boots. (Huge views to either side - the Isle of Wight is seen on a clear day.) On coming to the earth ramparts on the far side go down the steep slope half-left (yellow with cowslips in spring) to find a sturdy stile leading out of the fort area. A path leads alongside a wood and down to a bridle gate which takes you out of the Nature Reserve. An enclosed path continues.

At the end of the first field bear right and walk along the edge of a second field, curving left then right, and then taking a path through the centre of a woodland shaw. This eventually emerges onto a farm track which in turn leads to a concrete road. Almost immediately turn left on a stony track called Garden Hill Lane where a little brook runs clear along it. The brook becomes a lively, though not very boisterous, stream which we follow among trees all the way to the River Meon.

It seems strange, in retrospect, how this little brook brightened my day. Certainly the walk so far had been most enjoyable every step of the way, but the company of this fresh chalk stream was enough to raise my spirits even more. And why? It was a rarity on this walk, it is true, for chalk hills are jealous hills reluctant to show their streams, yet here was one that had found escape and I rejoiced with it as I considered its progress through the hills: first as moisture seeping into the rich downland turf, draining by way of grass roots, the root systems of flowers and shrubs and trees into the multi-layers of unseen chalk, percolating through that soft, cheese-like rock, passing hard blocks of flint that one distant day will no doubt be exposed to the winds. Slowly, persistently, the moisture trickled and dripped through the bosom of the hills until it met with the sticky resistance of a clay bed. There water was trapped until sufficient of it could force a means of escape. And the brook announced that escape, that release to sunshine and fresh air, with a chuckle and a swirl. No wonder it chuckled. And I rejoiced in its release too.

Jogging from one side to the other a narrow pathway follows the stream among the trees. In places it's something of a tight squeeze and a rucksack can easily be caught by low branches. And all the while the stream cuts a channel below. After half a mile of this you come to the embankment of a dismantled railway which you cross and continue ahead.

Note: *Those who plan to stay overnight in Droxford could bear left and follow the course of the old railway all the way to the village. Although not public right of way, I am assured that local people often use this as a foot-path. It is certainly preferable to following the road.*

Footbridge over the River Meon, near Exton

Out of the trees, but still beside the stream, the route crosses a farm track leading to Shavards Farm, then comes to a footbridge where the stream flows into the lovely River Meon. Bear left over the footbridge and the track takes you in a few paces to the A32 on the edge of Exton village. (West Meon lies some 2½ miles along the road to the right, Droxford about 2 miles to the left. There is a Post Office Stores beside the road in Corhampton, about one mile to the south, on the way to Droxford.)

Things Seen On The Way:

1: *Butser Hill Ancient Farm* has an interesting experiment in Iron Age agricultural methods, crops and materials. Ancient breeds of sheep (Soay) and cattle (Dexter) are kept here, and among the crops grown is a very early type of wheat known as einkorn. The main experimental site is not on the route of the SDW, but to the north of Butser Hill, while the very popular demonstration area is part of the Queen Elizabeth Country Park.

2: *Butser Hill* is not only the highest point on the South Downs, but is the site of ancient trackways, Bronze Age burial mounds, Celtic fields and defensive dykes. There is also evidence of Romano-British occupation here. On the summit stands a beacon that would have been lit in times of danger or of celebration, but this is dwarfed by the lofty telecommunications mast which, though no doubt beneficial to our modern society, is a great eyesore and one more piece of officially approved vandalism. From Butser Hill there is a justifiably renowned panorama which certainly attracts the crowds on bright days in summer. Do not expect to enjoy the views in solitude.

3: *Old Winchester Hill.* This prominent spur of downland was the site of Bronze Age barrows as well as an Iron Age hill fort. The outline of the fort is clearly evident and covers an area of about 14 acres. Huge views are just one of the rewards for gaining the summit. Much of the hilltop is National Nature Reserve, and there is a rich flora to enjoy. Nearby crosses the route of another long-distance footpath, that of King Alfred's Way (108 miles from Portsmouth to Oxford - Guidebook: *King Alfred's Way* by Laurence Main and Mark Richards, published by Thornhill Press).

Accommodation:

Droxford	Little Uplands Country Guest-House/Motel, Garrison Hill, Droxford, SO3 1QL. Tel: Droxford 878507
West Meon	Mrs. Wighton, Drake Cottage, West Meon, Petersfield, GU32 1LX. Tel: West Meon 327 Mr. Traill, The Court House, West Meon, Petersfield, GU32 1JG. Tel: West Meon 336 Mrs. Wilson, Brocklands Farm, West Meon, Petersfield, GU32 1JN. Tel: West Meon 228

Transport:

Exton has infrequent buses to Southampton and Petersfield (not Sundays). From *Droxford* buses go to Cosham station and Portsmouth (not Sundays).

SECTION 12:   **EXTON TO WINCHESTER**

Distance:	13 miles
Map:	O.S. Landranger series; Sheet 185 *Winchester & Basingstoke Area* 1:50,000
Accommodation:	Winchester - Hotels, Guest-houses, b&b, Youth Hostel

SECTION 12: EXTON TO WINCHESTER

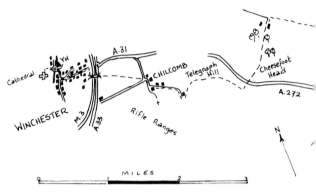

This final stage of the journey from Eastbourne provides a rich mixture of scenic pleasures. The landscape changes its pattern by the hour as you wander through it, and underfoot there is also plenty of variety as the route explores footpaths, tracks and quiet country lanes. Winchester hides itself from view virtually until the very last field path, while the heart of this historic city makes a worthy finish to a splendid long walk.

After leaving Exton the route heads roughly north-westwards climbing sharply to the Nature Reserve on Beacon Hill (yet another historic site). From there you pass the site of a lost village, cross the route of the Way-farer's Walk and take to a series of empty country roads and green lanes before coming onto Gander Down. This is a big open countryside, a spacious land of mellow hills and smiling valleys, but from it another green lane takes you into and alongside woodlands as far as Cheesefoot Head. The end of the walk is near, but there is one last stretch of downland that takes the route close to a military firing range. Happily the path avoids danger and drops from the escarpment through a sunken lane to tiny Chilcomb, and from there across one final field and into the streets of Winchester.

There are one or two alternative sections on offer here. The Countryside Commission's extension of the Way from Buriton to Winchester necessarily includes stretches of country lane where no bridleway exists, in order to enable riders to enjoy the full route as well as walkers. The walker, however, will be better advised to take alternative footpath routes in places,

84

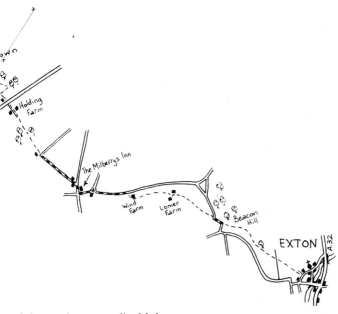

and these options are outlined below.

It would be possible to shorten the walk by use of private transport. There is a parking area beside the A272 at Cheesefoot Head (Grid ref: 529277) a few yards south-east of the South Downs Way, where cars could conveniently be left.

Refreshments may be had at The Millbury's Inn, about 5 miles from Exton.

* * *

Cross the A32 and take the minor road opposite into Exton village, bearing right to pass the 13th century parish church of St. Peter and St. Paul. (For refreshments at 'The Shoe' take the left-hand road just before reaching the church.) The road curves leftwards, and opposite a flint wall a track cuts back to the right immediately after passing Glebe Cottage. This brings you to an alternative option for walkers.

Walkers' Alternative Route: Bear right and walk along the track which brings you in a few paces to a stile set next to a field gate. Over the stile walk straight ahead parallel with the right-hand hedge until

85

you come to a second stile. This is on the right and it leads into a field which is crossed diagonally to the far corner. Over another stile maintain direction across a field to reach a farm track. Continue straight over this and into the next field where you cross the near right-hand corner to locate yet another stile near a metal water trough.

Continuing in the same direction cut across the near left-hand corner to a woodland shaw where another stile takes you to a very steep hillside. Maintain direction across the right-hand corner to find a stile about 30 yards up the slope. In the last steep hillside meadow there is little of a path to be seen, but the direction to make for is towards the top right-hand corner where a footpath signpost is seen beside a stile leading out to a country road. (This is where the official bridleway joins.) Do not go onto the road, but bear right and continue up the slope to the very topmost corner, cross horse bars and enter Beacon Hill National Nature Reserve. (1) Follow the left-hand fence, pass the trig point on Beacon Hill's summit (fine views) and continue along a clear track which takes you alongside woodlands and out by way of a bridle gate to a car park near the country road again. (Grid ref: 598227) You now rejoin the main bridle route.

SDW Bridleway from Exton to Beacon Hill: Ignore the track by Glebe Cottage and continue along the road in Exton, and soon after turn right at a junction and head out of the village (choosing right-hand options at all junctions) along White Way. This narrow lane winds among hedges for about a mile and a half to Beacon Hill. (It may be that a bridleway will be created across the meadow west of Beacon Hill's summit; if so, look for signs near the top of the hill. If not, remain on the road as described.) Just beyond Beacon Hill the lane comes to a T junction where you turn right and soon after there is a small car park on the right of the road on the edge of woodlands. The lane curves sharply left, and the two alternative routes converge once more.

Walk along the lane for a short distance with woods on your right. When it swings to the right leave the lane and walk straight ahead along a farm track. There are clumps of trees beside the track and in them on the right, half-hidden from view, a pond (Lomer Pond) surrounded by bluebells in spring. Soon after this the track passes a few grassy mounds off to the left - all that remains of the village of Lomer (although mentioned in the Domesday Book, the community died out in the Middle Ages - one of 90 such lost villages in Hampshire).

Little over a quarter of a mile beyond the abandoned village the track brings you to Lomer Farm. (It is better to walk between the buildings here on the continuing track, rather than fight a way through the undergrowth behind the cottages as per the map.) Immediately after passing the farm cottages the track curves to the left. Leave the track here and head off to the right, then bear left along another track going north-westwards along the edge of a large field. This track leads directly to Wind Farm and is shared by the route of the Wayfarer's Walk. (2)

Wind Farm is situated on the edge of woodlands. Bear right on a farm road to reach a country lane where you turn left. (The Wayfarer's Walk branches away from the lane over a stile, and from it there are lovely views to the north.) Follow the lane westwards for nearly a mile. There is a footpath, of sorts, on the right. On coming to a crossroads head to the right, and a few paces later pass The Millbury's Inn. (Grid ref: 570246) (The Mill Barrow nearby, shown on the O.S. map, marks the place where a windmill stood on a Bronze Age burial barrow. Millbury's is named after this.) Beyond the pub take the first turning on the left, a lovely quiet Hampshire lane ideal for cycling, tempting to spin a wheel for mile upon mile without constant fear of traffic. When the lane bends to the right near a Dutch barn, leave it and continue straight ahead along a farm track - another true green lane - for almost a mile. This is a lovely stretch of walking and it heads past Holding Farm and onto the A272 Petersfield to Winchester road.

Cross the road and continue ahead on a short tree-lined track which brings you to a field gate. Go through this and bear right to follow round the boundary hedge, bearing left in the far corner, still within the field but now heading north-west. Over the meadow brow join a vaguely sunken grass track which leads to a pair of successive field gates. Through the second of these you will see Ganderdown Farm huddling below to the left. Ahead stretches the broad rolling country-side of Gander Down; a breezy open landscape of big skies and unfolding panoramas. Maintain direction, pass beneath overhead power cables and join a clear track which aims north-westward lined with hedges.

My walk was drawing to a close but I was stangely reluctant to finish it. Around me the countryside spread itself in breeze-blown splendour. Peewits wheeled and cried and swooped one over another, gusting and playful, yet mournful too, with their sorrowing cry. Coming to a barn stocked with straw bales I settled myself out of the wind to eat my sandwiches and let the miles since Eastbourne shuffle themselves in my mind. It had been a grand walk - it still was - and my love for the ever-varied landscapes of Britain had grown stronger with each successive day. Now I stretched out comfortably and watched a puff of raincloud sweep my way. 'Precipitation in sight', as they say on the shipping forecast. It came, dampened the track, rattled on the barn roof and was gone again. Sunshine took over. A hare loped along the track and confronted a cock pheasant only a few feet from me. They stared at each other, then carried on with their own business, totally unaware that I was watching. The cock bird then caught sight of something of interest and strutted away, head projecting like an old Victorian spinster scurrying off to Mattins. Five minutes later a hen pheasant came out of the adjacent field through an open gateway and stood looking for her mate, squinting up and down. I was tempted to tell her where he'd gone, but decided to remain incognito and let the natural world continue around me, undisturbed by my presence. Who was I to interfere?

The hedge-lined track crosses a narrow lane and continues ahead for a further mile and a quarter until it comes to a crossing track with a farm set back on the left among trees. Turn left here and wander past the flint-walled cottage (there are barns on the right) and go into woods on a clear trail. Emerging from the woods soon after the track maintains direction beside a hedge, then through a bridle gate and onto an enclosed path that becomes a delightful avenue of beeches with Great Clump Woods stretching off to the left. This path brings you to the A272 at Cheesefoot Head, about 50 yards west of the car park.

Across the road another footpath leads for about 100 yards through a field to a cross-track. Turn right (remaining in the first field) and wander along the field edge beside trees and scrub to an enclosed continuing track. Approaching Telegraph Hill's tumulus the track leads between a plantation on the left and a field on the right, and beyond this the way curves a little leftwards and comes to a clear crossing track. (Grid ref: 517281) Turn left and follow this to a cottage; ahead is the boundary of Chilcomb rifle ranges, and there is often a red warning flag flying here.

Turn right on a narrow metalled lane that slopes downhill between high violet-studded banks leading to the little hamlet of Chilcomb. As the slope eases you will pass large corrugated barns on your right, and just beyond these note the lovely old black timbered grain store on staddle stones seen across the hedge.

On coming to a road junction bear right beside a flint wall. (The rather fine old church of Chilcomb stands at the end of the left-hand lane.) A few yards later you come to a Y shaped road junction with a stile directly ahead between the roads. Go up a few steps, over the stile and walk across the last field along a clear chalk track. It brings you to a footbridge leading over the A33 and M3, then the continuing tarmac path swings to the right on the outer edge of Winchester.

At a junction of paths turn left alongside trees and come to Petersfield Road. Walk straight ahead along this, passing All Saints Church on the left after some distance, and continue downhill with a flint wall on your right. Bear left at a junction into East Hill, and a few paces farther on head to the right at crossroads into Chesil Street. When you come to a roundabout turn left into the High Street (the Youth Hostel stands off to the right in Water Lane) and cross the bridge over the River Itchen to reach King Alfred's statue. Continue ahead into the main shopping area, then go left where signs indicate, to arrive by Winchester Cathedral.

The South Downs Way makes a fitting conclusion here.

A small city wrestling to find harmony between the old and the new, Winchester has so much of interest; historically, architecturally, spiritually. There's the famous College, founded in 1382; the fine old City Mill (owned by the National Trust and leased to YHA as a Youth Hostel); the lovely houses, archways, castle ruins, the Hospital of the Holy Cross. But the Cathedral is the most obvious, for this is the very heart and soul of Winchester. Graceful and at the same time a little severe on the outside, the interior is astonishingly beautiful. Sit there at the end of your walk and absorb the calm whispering glory that hangs in the air. The building was started in 1079, but as with all our ancient places of worship it belongs to many different periods of history. Each era added something inimitable. Today Winchester is Europe's longest cathedral. But it is more than that. Enter its peaceful sanctuary and be thankful for your days along the Downs.

Things Seen On The Way:

1: *Beacon Hill.* This is yet another site of an Iron Age hill fort. There are hut circles evident and signs of agricultural workings. There's also a causewayed ditch considered to be older even than the hill fort; Neolithic, perhaps. The summit of Beacon Hill is now a National Nature Reserve.

2: *Wayfarer's Walk.* This 70 mile long-distance path was developed by Hampshire County Council. It begins at Emsworth and finishes at Inkpen Beacon, crossing the route of the South Downs Way between Lomer Farm and Wind Farm. (Guidebook: *The Wayfarer's Walk* by Linda Herbst, published by Hampshire County Council.)

Accommodation:

Winchester   The Youth Hostel, The City Mill, 1 Water Lane, Winchester, SO23 8EJ. Tel: Winchester 53723

Mrs. Hennessey, Aquarius, 31 Hyde Street, Winchester, SO23 7DX. Tel: Winchester 54729

Mrs. Farrell, 5 Ranelagh Road, Winchester, SO23 9TA. Tel: Winchester 69555

Mrs. Dove, 28 Egbert Road, Hyde Street, Winchester, SO23 7EB. Tel: Winchester 61059

Mrs. Heathcote, 46 St. Cross Road, Winchester, SO23 9PS. Tel: Winchester 66539

For accommodation lists, write to:-

The Tourist Information Centre,
Guildhall,
The Broadway,
Winchester, SO23 9JZ

Public Transport:

Winchester has British Rail links with London, Portsmouth and Southampton. Also buses serving a number of different locations.

Plonk Barn, near Alfriston

SOUTH DOWNS WAY - EAST BOUND
(WINCHESTER TO EASTBOURNE)

For additional information on sites and scenes of particular interest, details of accommodation addresses, public transport etc., refer to parallel sections described earlier under West Bound Route.

SECTION 1:   **WINCHESTER TO EXTON**

Distance:	13 miles
Map:	O.S. Landranger series; Sheet 185 *Winchester & Basingstoke Area* 1:50,000
Accommodation:	Winchester - Hotels, Guest-houses, b&b, Youth Hostel
	Exton - None, but at -
	Droxford - Motel (2 miles off route)
	West Meon - Guest-house and b&b (2½ miles off route)

From the west door of Winchester Cathedral follow signs marked *Tourist information* as far as the High Street where you turn right and walk to King Alfred's statue, cross the bridge over the River Itchen and, at a roundabout, bear right into Chesil Street. Walk uphill until you come to a crossroads, and then turn left into East Hill. The road curves leftwards at a junction. Here take the right branch into Petersfield Road, soon passing All Saints Church on your right, and walk along this road for about half a mile to its end. A tree-lined footpath leads ahead. A few paces later bear right on another tarmac path which rises towards a footbridge leading over the M3 and A33. Cross the footbridge into a large field where a clear chalk track leads through. The Downs rise ahead, and it's now countryside nearly all the way to Eastbourne, a hundred miles away.

The chalk track brings you to a Y-shaped minor road junction on the edge of the little village of Chilcomb. Walk straight ahead and follow the narrow road as it veers right, then take the first turning on the left by a long flint wall. Follow this road as it passes a farm and climbs uphill, becoming a sunken lane between high banks. You will come to a notice warning of firing ranges, and here you turn left along a track to pass a cottage. Wander along this track for about a quarter

Old grain store at Chilcomb

of a mile, then bear right onto a continuing track leading along the edge of a field towards Telegraph Hill. The way curves to the right near the top of the hill, then goes alongside a small plantation. Follow the track for a further quarter of a mile, then turn left on a path cutting across the field to the A272 road at Cheesefoot Head. (Grid ref: 528278)

Cross the road and follow a continuing path that soon runs beside Great Clump Woods along a lovely avenue of beeches. A bridle gate leads out to a field and here you walk ahead following the right-hand hedge, come to a woodland and walk down a clear track. Out of the woods you pass a flint-walled cottage, continue a little farther, then reach a crossing track. Turn right and wander along this with steadily expanding views for about a mile and a quarter. You will come to a narrow country lane, cross straight ahead and continue on the hedge-lined track which leads onto Gander Down. The track ends, but you continue on grass, under overhead power cables and veering slightly to the left up a slope (Ganderdown Farm below to the right) come to a pair of successive field gates. Go through these and maintain direction, walking parallel with the left-hand hedge. On coming to the far side of this large meadow bear right, still along its left-hand boundary for a short distance. Then turn left through a field gate onto a tree-lined track. Walk down this to reach the A272 Winchester to Petersfield road again. (Grid ref: 561269)

Over the road continue along a farm drive, passing Holding Farm on the left, and keep on this as it becomes a track (a rather fine true green lane) for almost a mile. On reaching a solitary Dutch barn the track comes to a country lane. Maintain direction along this. When you come to a T junction bear right. Within a few yards you will reach The Millberry's Inn on the left. (Grid ref: 570246) (This is the only opportunity for refreshment before reaching Exton.)

Immediately beyond the pub there is a crossroads. Turn left and follow this lane for about three quarters of a mile. (After a short distance there is a path of sorts on the left of the lane.) Look for a flint farm road on the right just before Wind Farm, and walk along it a few paces, then turn left on a track behind outbuildings. This track becomes more obvious and leads straight ahead without deviation as far as Lomer Farm.

On emerging from the field-edge trail at Lomer Farm bear right just before the farm cottages to reach a clear track, then go left to wind round barns and right again on the original course heading south-eastwards. Keep along this track now, passing the site of an abandoned village (Lomer) on the right, and you will come to a country road. Maintain direction along this, with a wood on the left, and very shortly the road swings sharply to the right. There are now two options to face; one for walkers, the other being the bridle route.

Walkers' Alternative Route: Ignore the right-hand bend and walk ahead through an unmade car park, pass through a bridle gate and follow the track ahead alongside woodlands to reach Beacon Hill National Nature Reserve. Bear right past the trig point on the summit (splendid views), cross horse bars and follow the right-hand fence to a second set of bars. Cross these and maintain direction across the corner of a steeply sloping field to a woodland shaw. Another stile gives access into the trees, and beyond it the way cuts across the near corner to yet another stile in the hedge near a metal water trough. Continue in the same direction, reach a narrow farm track, cross it and over a stile maintain direction up the next field. On crossing the next stile bear left and follow the hedgerow to a short track which leads to a narrow road in Exton village. Bear left and follow it past the church (next turning on the right leads to The Shoe pub) keeping on this road until you reach the A32 on the outskirts of Exton.

SDW Bridleway from Beacon Hill to Exton: Keeping on the road ignore the unmade car park for Beacon Hill and swing to the right. In a few yards you come to a junction where you turn left (White Way). Ignore the next junction to the right and continue ahead. It's a narrow hedge-lined lane that winds downhill for about 1½ miles to Exton. On the edge of the village turn sharp left at a junction, and left again to curve through Exton, passing the church on the left, and coming to the A32 by the lovely River Meon. (Grid ref: 618212)

SECTION 2:   **EXTON TO BURITON**

Distance:	12½ miles
Maps:	O.S. Landranger series; Sheets 185 *Winchester & Basingstoke Area* and 197 *Chichester & The Downs* 1:50,000
Accommodation:	Buriton - b&b

Cross the A32 onto a track opposite. This leads to a footbridge over the delightful River Meon. A trail leads on a short distance and comes to a railway sleeper bridge. (The right-hand farm track leads to Shavards Farm.) A footpath follows the stream, in and out of trees and hedges, sometimes on the right bank, sometimes on the left. Keep alongside this, cross the embankment of a dismantled railway and continue on the streamside path. This eventually becomes a clear track (Garden Hill Lane) with the stream running along it. On coming to a crossing concrete farm road turn right and go through a gate. A track continues, then a footpath leads from it through the middle of a woodland shaw. On emerging from the trees bear left, then right alongside the fenced boundary of a large field. In the corner of the field turn left on a narrow path leading up to Old Winchester Hill National Nature Reserve.

The path climbs beside a wood and brings you to a stile. Over this a steep slope of flower-rich downland brings you onto the earth ramparts of an Iron Age hill fort. This is the crown of Old Winchester Hill and the views are extensive. Walk ahead through the centre of the hill fort, and at the far side go through a gate in the right-hand corner and follow the track ahead for about 400 yards. Before reaching the road bear left on a grass path which runs parallel with it. On your left the slope falls away to a tree-crowded combe and far-off lovely views hold your attention. Now work your way to the road and continue along it in the same direction as far as a junction. (The left fork goes down to Warnford, the continuing road leads to West Meon.)

Leave the road here and go through a gate on the right-hand side where a track slopes downhill diagonally to the right. Fine views overlook a broadening valley with stretches of downland ridge curving round. The track cuts through scrubby banks, and near the foot of the slope you bear left to come onto a concrete farm road leading to Whitewool Farm. Keep on the road as it veers leftwards behind attractive half-thatched outbuildings and follow the drive to a country road. Here turn right.

Walk along this road for about a quarter of a mile, and just after passing some cottages on the left, bear left on a clear concrete farm road leading between large fields. This brings you to a field with a grass trail leading ahead along the left-hand boundary. On the far side of the field go through a metal field gate and onto a bridleway enclosed by hedges. Turn right and walk along this for about a third of a mile. It then emerges from a tunnel of trees and hedges, veers left and brings you to a country road at Coombe Cross. (Grid ref: 667210)

Cross this road onto a continuing track which climbs onto Wether Down where there are two radio masts. Passing these on your left the track brings you to a public road by the buildings of HMS Mercury, the Naval School of Maritime Operations, Communications and Navigation. Turn left and follow the road as it leads through this inland establishment. On coming to crossroads keep ahead, and soon after you will reach a T junction. Opposite is a track bearing a sign: *'Unsuitable for Motor Vehicles'*. It will lead over Hyden Hill and Tegdown Hill, a fine green lane, first beside Hyden Wood, then over a more open landscape. After passing beneath a line of overhead power cables the track becomes surfaced by Homelands Farm. Shortly after you come to a minor crossroads and turn left.

A country road now takes you along the crest of the Downs towards the prominent telecommunications mast on Butser Hill, highest point on the South Downs. Ignore the side road which breaks away to the left, bound for East Meon, and continue towards the car park entrance for Butser Hill. Instead of going through the car park entrance cut ahead on a grass track, then through a bridle gate and along the line of the right-hand fence to descend from the hilltop. Go through another bridle gate and walk down the cropped downland slope towards the fenced area of Butser Hill Ancient Farm. Two bridle gates take you along the left-hand edge of the Ancient Farm demonstration site near the A3, then veer left to go under the busy road by an underpass that leads round to the Queen Elizabeth Country Park Centre.

Note: The Park Centre has interpretive displays, refreshments and toilets, and is well worth visiting.

Passing the Centre on your right walk ahead along a gravel path on the edge of Queen Elizabeth Forest, and come to a surfaced road. Bear left and follow the road until it makes a sharp curve at Benham's Bushes. Maintain direction, now along a flint track heading deeply into the forest. (Keep a lookout for deer.) The track leads to a picnic and barbecue site at Gravelhill Bottom, and you continue ahead, now going uphill. When you come to a crossing track bear left, then fork right to descend along the right-hand side of the forest. The track brings you to a bridle gate and out to a car parking area. Walk across this to a narrow road. (Grid ref: 734198) Buriton lies about half a mile down the road to the left.

SECTION 3:   **BURITON TO SOUTH HARTING (B2146)**

Distance:	3½ miles
Map:	O.S. Landranger series; Sheet 197 *Chichester & The Downs* 1:50,000
Accommodation:	South Harting - b&b

From the car park on the eastern edge of Queen Elizabeth Forest cross the Buriton to Chalton road and walk ahead along a metalled lane bordered by woods. The surfaced lane ends at Dean Barn where cottages with neat gardens stand on the right. A rutted track (muddy in places) leads ahead and winds on to Coulters Dean Farm where you once again join a metalled lane. Follow this as it bends left then right through Cockshott Wood, and by the entrance to Ditcham Park School bear left and continue along the lane to Sunwood Farm. The lane bends to the left and a few paces later you must leave it to take a track on the right beside a house. This track is known as Forty Acre Lane, and a few paces after joining it you leave Hampshire and enter West Sussex.

Follow Forty Acre Lane as it heads a little south of east (ignoring alternative paths) as far as a narrow crossing lane. Walk straight ahead to rejoin the track between cottages, and continue ahead for almost a mile until you come to the B2146 road. (Grid ref: 783185) (Immediately before it a path on the left leads down to South Harting for refreshments and/or accommodation.)

SECTION 4:   **SOUTH HARTING TO COCKING**

Distance:	7½ miles
Map:	O.S. Landranger series; Sheet 197 *Chichester & The Downs* 1:50,000
Accommodation:	Cocking - b&b

St. Martha's Hill where the Downs Link begins

Cross the B2146 road south of the village of South Harting, and onto the track opposite. This rises steadily among trees of an area known as The Bosom, reaches the B2141 and on the other side of the road you pass along the edge of a car park and picnic site and wander ahead along the edge of the escarpment of Harting Downs. Views from here are very fine. Wander along the main trail crossing the Downs, and on the eastern side go through an area of scrub and then descend into the head of a soft green valley; Bramshott Bottom. You will come to cross-tracks with a signpost. Ahead rises Beacon Hill (the second so-named on the route since leaving Winchester). Turn right at the signpost and take the track which leads round the slopes of Beacon Hill a little above the valley. The track becomes scrub-lined and takes you to a spinney in the corner of a field south of Beacon Hill. Bear sharp left and wander along the continuing track which now heads north along the right-hand side of the field. It then curves to the right above a combe known as Millpond Bottom, descends to a saddle and then climbs steeply up to Pen Hill. (Grid ref: 812183)

From the summit of Pen Hill there are more fine views. The way then leads down the left-hand edge of a field towards a wood where you bear right, over a crossing path and along the edge of a spinney. An enclosed track leads on to a bridle gate. Through this you come to a narrow farm track with Buriton Farm seen huddling in a hollow to the right. Bear left on the track for a few paces, then head to the right along another rough track climbing south towards Philliswood Down.

Ignore alternatives and remain along the main track with a fence on your right as you enter woodlands. When you come to cross-tracks on the edge of the wood, turn left, soon to pass on your left a series of five ancient tumuli known as the Devil's Jumps. The track now has a high fence on the right. Beyond it, but mostly hidden by the trees, stands the curious Monkton House. You will no doubt hear the screeching of peacocks from the grounds of the house.

Emerging from the tree shade the way heads across fenced meadows over Didling Hill, but towards Linch Down there is much arable, with extensive woods off to the right. Between Linch Down and Cocking Down it is possible to see the spire of Chichester Cathedral way off to the right, and even the Solent and the Isle of Wight in the far distance. The route is clear and broad, and after Cocking Down the chalk track steadily descends to Middlefield Lane, passes a farm and reaches the A286 Midhurst to Singleton road (Grid ref: 875166) about half a mile south of Cocking.

SECTION 5: **COCKING TO AMBERLEY STATION**
(Arun Valley)

Distance: 11 miles
Map: O.S. Landranger series; Sheet 197 *Chichester & The Downs* 1:50,000
Accommodation: Amberley - b&b
Houghton - b&b
Warningcamp - Youth Hostel (Arundel) (3 miles off route)

Middlefield Lane brings the walker off Cocking Down to the A286 road a little south of Cocking village. On the eastern side of the road a matching track, Hillbarn Lane, continues the route onto Manorfarm Down. Walk ahead up the track of Hillbarn Lane and very soon you will pass Hill Barn Farm. On the right-hand side of the track here there is a water tap provided for walkers. Between this point and the A27 (end of Section 9) several such supplies of drinking water have been provided specifically for South Downs Way walkers and riders.

Follow the flint track all the way up to Manorfarm Down and go through a gate with woods on the right. Continue ahead, following along the right-hand side of a large field with a trig point and timber-built hunting platform standing in the centre of it. At the far end of the field the way enters woodland and curves first left then right. On the left is Heyshott Down archaeological site. The route is clear through the woods, but it can be rather muddy in places, especially over Graffham Down. Other tracks and pathways lead off to left and right, but the main track is obvious and it leads either through, or alongside, woods for three miles or so maintaining a regular course along the top of the Downs. Because of the woodlands there are practically no distant views and the walker must look for other pleasures. (Keep alert for sign of deer.)

After emerging from the woods a lengthy stretch takes you along the edge of arable land on Woolavington Down. (Fields on the left, woodlands on the right.) At the end of this stage there is a large signpost with routes heading left to Duncton and right to East Dean. Continue ahead to pass through a short section of woodland and out to a sloping field. Should this field have been recently ploughed and no sign of footpath being visible, take a rough bearing on the aerial masts seen on Burton Down ahead. The route of the path leads to a bridle gate in a mid-field fence, and through this descends towards the bottom right-

The Old Farm, Houghton

hand corner of the field where you join a broad track (at a junction of tracks) and continue ahead downhill among trees and grassy banks. This leads to the A285 Petworth to Chichester road beside Littleton Farm. (Grid ref: 951144)

Cross the road and wander ahead on the continuing track which winds uphill among hedges, trees and flower-bright banks towards Burton Down. Through the edge of the woods, then over arable land the track wanders on. A passage among yew trees marks Burton Down and you continue through National Trust property with the aerial masts standing off to your left. After passing the aerials you come to a crossing track and bear left (on the route of the Roman Stane Street) for a short distance. Then turn right at the next junction to follow a clear track to a car parking area marked with a large signpost bearing directions to Noviomagus (Chichester), Bignor and Londinium (London).

The route maintains direction ahead following a fence on the right. Crossing Bignor Hill (737 feet) you come to a bridle gate beside a memorial mounting block - Toby's Stone. There are broad views from here, with Chanctonbury Ring signalling ahead in the east. Descending now beside a fence you come to cross-tracks and continue ahead, soon to drop steeply winding among scrub to some black barns.

99

Passing these to your left follow the confined track curving ahead to the right over Westburton Hill. Off to the right stretch the extensive woodlands of Houghton Forest.

The chalk track leads clearly on heading south-eastwards. It goes towards the edge of woods, then veers away to reach the A29 road a mile or so south of the village of Bury. Turn right and walk along the road for about 100 yards, then bear left along another track descending beside Coombe Wood. Beyond the wood, with views ahead over the valley of the River Arun, the track winds to the right, then left, and comes onto a narrow country lane. Bear right and follow this into Houghton village. (Refreshments and accommodation available.)

On arriving in Houghton's main street (the B2139) turn left and walk with caution along it, over the bridge crossing the Arun and, a few yards later, come to Amberley railway station. (Refreshments available at tea rooms near the bridge and at the Bridge Inn. There is a water tap outside the pub. Accommodation in Amberley village a short walk to the north, and at Arundel Youth Hostel by a 3 mile walk, or by train followed by 1 mile walk. Details under Section 7 of the West Bound route description.)

SECTION 6:   **AMBERLEY STATION TO WASHINGTON**

Distance:	6½ miles
Maps:	O.S. Landranger series; Sheets 197 *Chichester & The Downs* and 198 *Brighton & The Downs* 1:50,000
Accommodation:	Washington - Hotel, b&b (1 mile off route)

Walk along the B2139 road beyond Amberley station for about 400 yards. On the right you will see a minor road (High Titton Lane) breaking away. Take this lane and follow as it rises steadily between hedges that disguise deep-cut chalk quarries on either side. On coming to a T junction bear right for about 80 yards, then go left along an enclosed path climbing the hillside towards Amberley Mount. Keeping Downs Farm well to your right pass through a gate and continue uphill alongside a fence to another gate and onto a clear track that adheres to the northern edge of the Downs. Fine views overlook the water-cut flatlands below.

Along this easy track you pass a number of ancient burial mounds. Beyond Rackham Banks you go through a small woodland and the fenced route leads on over Springhead Hill, with clumps of trees and hedges and a spread of arable farmland on the right. There's a small parking area beyond Springhead Hill with a minor road leading left towards Storrington, and about a mile beyond this another road also drops to the north. Here you will find the Chantry Post (a large signpost subject to vandalism), a couple of seats and fine views north over the Weald.

The route continues straight ahead beyond the Chantry Post, now across grass and running parallel with the right-hand fence, over Sullington Hill and on to a large Dutch barn. Just past this the track forks. Take the left branch and wander on to Barnsfarm Hill where there is another junction of tracks. (If you plan to stay overnight in Washington, take the left-hand track.) If you plan to continue, walk ahead on the descending flint track through broad fields with big views. On reaching a tree-shaded section maintain direction and the track becomes a surfaced narrow lane with a few houses beside it. On the way down you will see another water supply on the right of the lane. Soon after the lane curves to the right and brings you to the busy A24 a little south of Washington village. (Grid ref: 119118).

SECTION 7: **WASHINGTON TO BOTOLPHS (Adur Valley)**

Distance:	6½ miles
Maps:	O.S. Landranger series; Sheet 198 *Brighton & The Downs* 1:50,000
Accommodation:	Bramber - Hotel (1 mile off route)
	Truleigh Hill - Youth Hostel (2 miles ahead on continuing route)

The A24 London to Worthing road is an extremely busy one and great caution must be exercised when crossing. On the eastern side take the old road heading left towards Washington village, and a few yards along this take a track running parallel with the old road. The track forks a few paces later. Take the right branch now heading east to climb the slopes of hillside that will lead to Chanctonbury Ring. The track is of rough flints, bordered here and there by hedges and scrub, and on coming to a major junction you must bear left and wander round the hill to go through a bridle gate by a cattle-grid (a dew pond on the left) and onto the green hilltop meadow crowned by the beech clump of Chanctonbury Ring. Pass along the right-hand (southern) side of the trees where the clear trail swings across the greensward to a gateway. Soon after this you come to another junction of tracks. (Left towards woods and down into the Weald, while the right-hand track is the major route linking Chanctonbury with Cissbury Ring. We take neither of these routes.) Cross over and walk south-eastwards on a clearly defined track with woods off to the left and arable on the right. There are other paths cutting away, but sufficient waymarks and signposts make the South Downs Way obvious. Over Steyning Round Hill (trig point in the field on the right) you come to a crossing bridleway and continue ahead, soon reaching a minor road winding along the very crest of the Downs. (Grid ref: 163096)

Maintain direction to walk south along the road for half a mile. Just prior to the road bending to the right you will see a field gate on the left. Go through this and follow the left-hand fence as the path slopes downhill with the soft combe of Steyning Bowl to the left. You reach a fenced area containing a little plantation of trees known as Bramber Beeches (commemorating the diamond jubilee of the West Sussex Federation of Women's Institutes in 1979). The way heads to the right and climbs to a metal field gate on the left. Go through this where a track leads across Annington Hill with views unfolding around you. (The sea now coming into view, and the delightful combe of Winding Bottom below on the right.)

The track descends, passes a rickety cattle shelter and approaches Tinpots Cottage. Here the way swings left and leads through trees down to a quiet country road in the little hamlet of Botolphs. Now bear right and walk down the road, passing Annington Old House and Annington Farm. The road then approaches the lovely little St. Botolph's Church, and curves to the right just before it. At this curve turn left through a gateway and a few yards later come onto the route of the Downs Link. (Grid ref: 194094)

SECTION 8: **BOTOLPHS TO PYECOMBE**

Distance:	7½ miles
Map:	O.S. Landranger series; Sheet 198 *Brighton & The Downs* 1:50,000
Accommodation:	None on route, but at -
	Hassocks - Hotel (1½ miles off route)
	Patcham - Youth Hostel (2½ miles off route)

From the junction of the South Downs Way with the Downs Link between Botolphs and the River Adur, continue on the clear track to the riverside, then bear right to reach the footbridge erected especially for the South Downs Way. Cross the river and a few paces beyond you will come to a drinking water supply and a seat. The path swings to the left and brings you onto the A283 road. Cross this with care and turn left to walk alongside the road for nearly 150 yards when you come to a field gate on the right giving access to a fence-enclosed track climbing the slopes of Beeding Hill. Near the top of this you go through another gate and over meadowland to a bridle gate. Through the bridle gate you come onto a green lane with a track leading in from the left. Here you will find an attractive fingerpost erected by the Society of Sussex Downsmen.

Walk straight ahead on the lane/track heading onto the crest of the Downs. There is a footpath in the grass to the left of this. It brings you directly to Truleigh Hill Youth Hostel (Grid ref: 220105) and the way continues ahead to pass a farm or two and an untidy collection of buildings and aerials on the crown of the hill. Over this the scene is more open and pleasing. The track becomes a broad chalk way, looks into the spacious Weald, crosses Edburton Hill and is confronted by a string of high power cables and their marching line of pylon skeletons.

Go under the power lines where there are cross-tracks (north to Fulking, south through the heart of the Downs to Southwick and the sea) and climb Perching Hill. Fulking Hill comes next, with fine views. The embankments of Devil's Dyke hill fort are clearly seen ahead, as is the much-visited Devil's Dyke Hotel. Going through a bridle gate cross a grassy meadow well away from the right-hand fence to find another bridle gate which gives onto a narrow road leading to the hotel. Cross the road and continue ahead along a well-trodden track through scrub and trees to reach a grassy car parking area. (Sadly this is often a litter-strewn place.) Veer leftwards on the lower edge of this open grass space and descend past a covered reservoir to the road at Saddlescombe; a tiny hamlet on the north side of the road. (Grid ref: 271114)

Cross the road and take the track which leads past a cottage on the right and comes onto a farm track. Now follow this between barns and cottages and onto a hedge-lined path through a bridle gate. The way becomes a little sunken as it climbs, then passing through another bridle gate a steep grass slope takes you up to West Hill following beside a fence on the right. A bridleway leads over the hilltop and you can see the Clayton Windmills (Jack and Jill) on the far hill. (The next section of the walk leads past them.)

On coming to a junction of tracks bear left and descend to a narrow farm drive, past riding stables and a few yards later you will reach the busy A23 Brighton road opposite the Plough Inn at Pyecombe. (Grid ref: 292124)

SECTION 9:   **PYCOMBE TO NEWMARKET INN (A27)**

Distance:	8½ miles
Map:	O.S. Landranger series; Sheet 198 *Brighton & The Downs* 1:50,000
Accommodation:	None on route

Pyecombe is marooned by the A23 and A273, but the Downs rise on all sides and it does not take long to escape the noise of traffic and the smell of exhaust fumes. With caution cross the A23 towards the Plough Inn and walk along Church Lane which goes uphill along the right-hand side of the pub. On reaching the church turn right into School Lane and, just before coming onto the A273, bear left along a narrow bush-lined path. This brings you out opposite the entrance to Pyecombe Golf Club.

Cross the road and walk up the track, passing the golfers' car park, then wandering alongside the delightfully situated golf course itself. Near the head of the slope you come to crossing tracks about 100 yards south of New Barn Farm. Bear left and walk between farm buildings with the Jack and Jill windmills a short distance ahead. The track leads within a few yards of them, but at a junction you must turn right, away from the windmills, on a clear track steadily going up onto the crest of the Downs.

The route leads along the northern edge of the escarpment and passes the so-called Keymer Post (much vandalised, as the Chantry Post earlier) where you leave West Sussex and enter East Sussex. (The village of Keymer lies some distance to the north on the course of one of several Roman roads that traverse the region.) Beyond the Keymer Post the way continues for a further mile or so to reach the much-visited Ditchling Beacon (813 feet), a renowned viewpoint and one of the highest points of the South Downs. (It is the highest of the Sussex Downs.) Passing the trig point to your right you come to a car park (there is usually an ice-cream van here). Cross the Ditchling to Brighton road and take the higher of two tracks ahead. Follow the right-hand fence and walk ahead with enticing views north into the

Weald, pass the isolated Streathill Farm and continue across Plumpton Plain on a clear farm track.

About 2½ miles east of Ditchling Beacon you come to a crossing track and turn right among bushes and with a wood to your right. The track is confined by hedge and fence and half a mile or more later, on reaching a junction of bridleways, you turn left and pass beneath overhead power cables. A flint track leads through an open countryside of arable farmland on Balmer Down. It is a lengthy section that takes you down to a small woodland, Ashcombe Plantation (Grid ref: 382094). A path takes you through the wood, emerging by a flint wall at a wooden gate. Turn right and follow a sunken track down to an embankment overlooking the A27 road. Go down the bank and, with great care, cross over to the Newmarket Inn. (There's a water tap outside the petrol station to the right of the pub.)

SECTION 10: **NEWMARKET INN TO RODMELL**

Distance:	5½ miles
Map:	O.S. Landranger series; Sheet 198 *Brighton & The Downs* 1:50,000
Accommodation:	Rodmell - Guest-house, b&b
	Telscombe - Youth Hostel (2 miles off route)

Between the Newmarket Inn and the filling station a lane heads beneath a railway arch and becomes a track going uphill through gates and alongside the woods of Newmarket Plantation. Above the woods you go through a bridle gate heading leftwards and continue uphill to, a second bridle gate. Now follow the left-hand fence to a crossing track (Juggs Road) where you turn left through yet another bridle gate and into a large sweep of meadow. Wander ahead through the meadow, keeping near the right-hand fence until over the crest where you make for the far left corner. There you will come to a pond and a gate. There are large views ahead overlooking Lewes and the Downs towards Ditchling Beacon.

Go through the gate and bear half-right (there's little in the way of a track to be seen) across another meadowland and pass along the right-hand side of Kingston Hill dew pond). (Grid ref: 383078) A short distance beyond this go through another gate and come to a saddle with crossing tracks. (A fine view right into a lovely little combe, and left down to Kingston-near-Lewes. Ahead the downland slopes sweep into the Weald.)

Walk ahead along the upper edge of the slope to follow the right-hand fence along Swanborough Hill on one of the finest stretches of the South Downs Way. At the end of a long downland section blocked by a fence, go through a gate on the right and walk up the slope for about 60 yards, then bear left on a concrete farm road. This leads in a die-straight course through open fields over Iford Hill and Front Hill. After about a mile of this you go through a gate and continue ahead along a track that becomes a path beside trees and hedges at Mill Hill. When this brings you to the entrance to a house on the right, bear left and follow Mill Lane down to Rodmell. (Grid ref: 418059)

SECTION 11: **RODMELL TO ALFRISTON**

Distance:	8 miles
Maps:	O.S. Landranger series; Sheets 198 *Brighton & The Downs* and 199 *Eastbourne, Hastings & Surrounding Area* 1:50,000
Accommodation:	Alfriston - Hotels, b&b, Youth Hostel

On coming to the main street in Rodmell turn right and follow the road for half a mile before breaking off to the left on a tree-shrouded lane that leads into the hamlet of Southease. (About 250 yards before turning off for Southease there is a track leading away to the right through the quiet valley of Cricketing Bottom. This leads to Telscombe for the Youth Hostel.)

Follow the lane down into Southease and passing the ancient church and village green to your right continue on, cross the River Ouse and walk to Southease station. Over the railway line keep along the road to Itford Farm and the A26. Cross the road, bear right and a few paces later take a chalk and flint track on the left that makes a long winding curve up the steep slopes of Itford Hill. Initially the track curves right, then bends leftwards. A vague grass trail now breaks away to the left and ascends parallel with the right-hand fence to the top of the hill. Veer to the right and follow a much more evident track, still alongside the fence, and pass a trig point on the left standing on a grassy bank containing a dried-up dew pond (Red Lion Pond; Grid ref: 446055).

Following the right-hand fence the grass path leads towards radio masts on Beddingham Hill. Shortly before reaching these you cross a narrow metalled road and continue on a clear track along the left-hand side of the masts to reach a car parking area with its access road coming from West Firle. Wander through the car park and out by way of a bridle gate on the left onto the open edge of a downland slope. Keeping to the ridge follow the right-hand fence heading east towards Firle Beacon, then curve a little to the right by some tumuli to reach the trig point on the summit of the hill (713 feet).

Views have been very fine to Firle Beacon, and they continue to be so practically all the way to Alfriston. A track leads on from the trig point, heading south-east now and passing various hummocks of tumuli, it curves round the hill and descends to a second car park and picnic area (popular with hang-gliding enthusiasts) below Bostal Hill. Through a pair of gates the route continues ahead and climbs Bostal Hill, beyond which the fence starts to veer away to the right while you maintain direction ahead on grass, and over a green brow to reach a bridle gate next to a kissing gate.

A clear flint track leads on along the very crest for a mile or more with broad panoramas to enjoy. On coming to a junction of paths continue on descending now among bushes towards Alfriston, then with a fence on the left the track broadens, leads to a surfaced residential street and, over minor crossroads, brings you to Alfriston High Street beside the Star Inn (Grid ref: 520031).

SECTION 12: **ALFRISTON TO EASTBOURNE (via The Seven Sisters)**

Distance:	12 miles
Map:	O.S. Landranger series; Sheet 199 *Eastbourne, Hastings & Surrounding Area* 1:50,000
Accommodation:	Eastbourne - Hotels, b&b, Youth Hostel (Beachy Head)

It should be noted that this stage of the route is footpath only, and riders should follow Section 12(a), the inland route via Jevington. There is little to choose between the two for scenic grandeur, and walkers with sufficient time are encouraged to walk both routes - perhaps out to Eastbourne via the Seven Sisters, and back to Alfriston by the inland route. (See Section 1(a) of the West Bound Route for description of this return stage.)

From the Star Inn bear right along the High Street for a few yards, then go left down an alleyway past the United Reformed Church, then with the village green and Parish Church of St. Andrew on the right, continue on the path to cross a white-railed footbridge over the River Cuckmere. The path leads on and comes to a narrow road opposite the converted Plonk Barn, but before coming to this it is better to take the footpath leading to the right along the edge of a field, coming to the road a little farther on. Then you skirt a small pond, still on footpath, and continue along it towards Litlington. Walk through the village, passing the church on your right, then The Plough and Harrow pub (a footpath just before this leads across the river to Alfriston Youth Hostel) and then cross the road to the left into a minor lane and go through a kissing gate on the right.

Go up the hill and make for a stile in the top left-hand corner of the field. Over this continue ahead following a fence and crossing more stiles before dropping down towards woodlands in Charleston Bottom. (Behind the trees to the right is Charleston Manor.) The path in Charleston Bottom is enclosed and it takes you to a series of steps leading up into Friston Forest. At the top of the steep incline there's another stile and over this you walk ahead along a ride, then bear left onto a broad track contouring above some houses. At a junction of tracks turn right and go down to a road which leads into the charming hamlet of West Dean.

You come to a duck pond at a T junction. Cross the road and pass to the left of the pond on a clear track which brings you to a flight of more than two hundred steps climbing once more into Friston Forest. A path leads on through the trees and soon comes to a low wall with a built-in stile. Ahead the windings of the river can be seen snaking off to Cuckmere Haven and the sea.

Cross the stile and descend the steep meadow to farm buildings at Exceat and onto the A259 road. Bear right and walk along the road towards Exceat Bridge, but just before it go left onto a riverside footpath and follow the Cuckmere towards the sea. Near Cuckmere Haven, but before coming to the stony beach, take the raised path heading to the cliffs on the left. A steep chalk track leads onto the first of the Seven Sisters, (Haven Brow) and then you continue eastwards up and down along the clifftop with the sea far below to the right. Do not stray too close to the cliff edge. Because of erosion the edges are frequently crumbling away.

Over each successive Sister the path leads to Birling Gap where there are several buildings (refreshments and toilets), and you go through a car park and continue on the eastern side to climb now towards the former lighthouse at Belle Tout. Bear left round the wall that encloses it, then maintain direction down a tarmac path towards the road, which here makes a sharp bend. Beachy Head lighthouse is seen clearly from this point. Continue up the grassy clifftop path to the brow of Beachy Head which has a cluster of buildings and dramatic views down to the lighthouse way below. (Refreshments and toilets nearby.)

After Beachy Head an asphalt path (later unsurfaced) takes you down to Heathy Brow, then round the rim of Whitbread Hole and its playing field. On grass now among scrub the way steepens to the official end of the South Downs Way at Holywell on the edge of Eastbourne.

For a more logical conclusion continue down to the seafront and walk along the lower promenade, past the Wish Tower (a converted Martello Tower) to Eastbourne Pier. (Grid ref: 617989)

From Winchester Cathedral to Eastbourne Pier; a walk of many delights. I hope you enjoyed it as much as I did.

SECTION 12(a): **ALFRISTON TO EASTBOURNE**
(Inland route via Jevington)

Distance:	9 miles
Map:	O.S. Landranger series; Sheet 199 *Eastbourne, Hastings & Surrounding Area* 1:50,000
Accommodation.	Eastbourne - Hotels, b&b, Youth Hostel (Beachy Head)

Although this is the bridleway route to Eastbourne, it also makes a very fine walk in its own right and is highly recommended. From the Star Inn bear left along Alfriston High Street to the Market Cross and, immediately before it, turn right into a narrow lane which goes towards the river. Then turn right on a track in front of some cottages heading towards the Parish Church, and bear left to cross a white-railed bridge over the Cuckmere.

On coming to a narrow lane in front of the converted Plonk Barn turn left and follow along it for about 400 yards. (Beware of traffic.) You will then reach a road junction and the way now heads to the right along a track that becomes sunken between bushes and trees and comes to a country lane leading from Wilmington. (Grid ref: 532033) Cross this and continue to climb on a clear broad track that passes an underground reservoir and winds round the head of a combe (Ewe Dean) to emerge onto the Downs at Windover Hill. (Magnificent views.) All around are ancient earthworks, burial barrows and ditches, and the remains of flint mines dating from the Stone Age. This is one of the most interesting of the many archaeological sites on the South Downs. Below, unseen, England's largest chalk figure, the Long Man of Wilmington, is etched in the hillside.

A somewhat rutted trail leads past the summit of Windover Hill, goes through a gate in a grassy saddle and onto a very large meadow. Bear right to cross this, passing well above the combe of Deep Dean, and maintain direction to approach the ruined walls of Hill Barn seen beyond the far left fence. Before reaching the fence veer a little more to the right and find a bridle gate with a clear grassy path leading among trees and bushes to a second gate. Through this, at a junction of tracks, turn left on a descending track among the little woods of Jevington Holt. Near the end of the woods the farm track curves leftwards and on the right you will see a path heading down among more trees. There is a fence on the left and soon another on the right with a pasture beyond it. The path leads directly to Jevington church.

Passing the church on your left a lane takes you into Jevington's village street. (For refreshments at the Eight Bells pub, turn left for a short distance.) Bear right and walk along the street for a few yards, then head to the left along a sunken lane that becomes a rough track climbing among trees, bushes and flowers onto the Downs once more. This takes you onto Willingdon Hill (660 feet) where you come to cross-tracks and interesting stone markers. Continue ahead, following the easy track along the crest of the Downs with Eastbourne seen below to the left. You will cross Eastbourne Downs Golf Course and reach the A259 Eastbourne to Brighton road. (Those requiring Beachy Head Youth Hostel should turn off left here. The hostel is found about a third of a mile downhill.)

Cross the road and maintain direction along a grass track, curving slightly leftwards. At a fork, take the left branch to descend among scrub, then passing a domed reservoir on the left among trees you will soon reach the rather untidy and unsatisfactory official end to the South Downs Way.

Paradise Drive stretches ahead. Go along this and at a junction bear half-right into Gaudick Road which you follow to the far end. Go over a crossing road into Milnthorpe Road, then left along Chesterfield Road as far as King Edward's Parade with the sea beyond. Cross ahead and onto a path leading to a landscaped circular mound with seats placed around it. Bear left here and walk along the surfaced path beside flower beds and neat lawns, past the Wish Tower (a converted Martello Tower) and along the promenade to Eastbourne Pier. This is a more fitting end to the walk from Winchester than the rather unloved spot beyond Paradise Drive.

Downs Link signpost

THE DOWNS LINK

THE DOWNS LINK

The concept of a trans-Weald walking route to link the North and South Downs is an interesting and popular one. In the east the Wealdway does just that on its journey from Gravesend on the Thames to Beachy Head; so does the Vanguard Way which strikes south from suburban East Croydon on a 62-mile course to Seaford Head. To the west the Wey-South Path similarly links the two lines of the Downs by following various waterways from Guildford in Surrey to the River Arun near Amberley in West Sussex. But the Downs Link is the only route that makes a conscious effort to join the two officially approved long distance downland Ways in this part of the country.

The Downs Link is not one of the Countryside Commission's approved National Long Distance Paths, nor is it a result of the enthusiasm of a group of ramblers. It is, in fact, a joint development completed in 1984 by three local authorities: West Sussex and Surrey County Councils and Waverley Borough Council based at Godalming in Surrey. Between them, these three authorities own much of the former railway lines along which the path runs for the greater part of its 33-mile journey. The remainder of the route follows existing footpaths or bridleways (and a small stretch of country lane) that conveniently join the paths of the old railway, thus completing an easy-to-follow recreational walking or riding route from St. Martha's Hill on the North Downs Way outside Guildford, to the hamlet of Botolphs where the River Adur breaches the wall of the South Downs between Steyning and Shoreham-by-Sea.

As with the South Downs Way, the Downs Link is bridleway throughout. By far the majority of the route is easy underfoot, mostly firm and, because of its railway origins, maintaining a level course through cuttings and along embankments where the surrounding land rises and falls over natural hillside features. It is also remarkably straight - though not at all uninteresting to follow as might be assumed. Waymarking at all major crossing tracks is exemplary, so one is not likely to be called upon to exercise navigational skills with map and compass whilst tackling this route, thereby leaving the walker to amble along at a leisurely pace that makes it possible to experience the full luxury and variety of the countryside of southern England without constant reference to the map.

This is a walk that will repay a leisurely attitude of mind as you wander through a landscape surprisingly empty of towns or major road systems. A walk through a southern back-country devoid perhaps of scenic drama, but certainly not lacking in interest. By its very nature the Downs Link provides plenty of opportunities for short walks from neighbouring villages, or by the use of a motorised back-up support. But for those who enjoy the challenge of a long walk, it could be broken into a two-day outing, ideal for a weekend jaunt or, for the extra-energetic, a very long day's stride. By whichever method you tackle it, you'll find along the way a rich quota of wildlife and constantly changing vegetation and soil types with all the bounty that entails.

The route does not actually begin on the North Downs proper, but on the Greensand Ridge which runs parallel with them, as an inner lining, so to speak, to the Downs. The sandy, acid soil of the greensand is heavily wooded with oak, beech, pine and hawthorn; with thickets of hazel and hedgerows spiky with holly. Below, in the Tillingbourne Valley, there are streams and boggy patches lined with alder and willow, and along their margins plants that exploit damp places. Heading south the land rises to a minor ridge, again heavily wooded but with patchy heaths bright with gorse and springy with heather. Birch and pine dominate the woods here.

Through the Weald clay lies heavy, but along the track and in path-side spinneys there is an abundant flora - especially in spring. Wild garlic and bluebells throw a dazzle of white on blue around the base of so many woodland trees, while later, as you near the South Downs, so violets, then cowslips and early purple orchids will catch the eye.

All these changes become evident to the walker on his journey south. But what of the route itself? What of its history?

* * *

When the railways of Britain were nationalised in 1948, the newly formed company took on a network amounting to 19,000 miles of track; by 1967 that network had been stripped to 11,000 miles following the closure of numerous unprofitable branch lines. Along some of those 8,000 miles of unwanted line a number of recreational footpaths and bridleways have been created, of varying lengths and through diverse stretches of countryside. The Downs Link is one of them.

The railway whose demise makes this walk a practical reality was created in two parts. In 1861 the first section running inland from Shoreham to Itchingfield Junction (about 2 miles south-west of

Horsham) was opened by the London-Brighton South Coast Railway. (This linked with the Horsham main line which is still much in use today.) The second, northern, section followed four years later and was built by the Horsham and Guildford Direct Railway Company. This ran from Christ's Hospital (near Itchingfield Junction) to Guildford in the hope of becoming a major through-route between the South Coast and the Midland towns. That aspiration never materialised as a practical reality and throughout its hundred years in existence the line never attracted more than local traffic. Dr. Beeching's 1963 report into the viability of Britain's railway network effectively killed the route, and by 1966 both lines had closed.

Today, as you wander along the Downs Link, there are various signs giving evidence of this former railway. Not only the obvious alignment of the bed, with its cuttings and embankments, but numerous brick-built bridges crossing the line - some carrying motor traffic, some now disused and overgrown. There are one or two signals left standing; a lonely platform, an obvious siding, a station sign where no station stands today. One station remains in immaculate pristine condition, however, but that is now a private residence.

To the railway buff, the Downs Link will have considerable appeal.

* * *

As has been stated before, the route begins outside Guildford on the lofty viewpoint of St. Martha's Hill on the Greensand Ridge. From there it drops into the Tillingbourne Valley, over Blackheath and round the edge of Chinthurst Hill to meet the course of the railway by a stretch of the Wey and Arun Canal. A tributary of the River Wey snakes alongside the path for a while; then alongside Cranleigh and into fields and woods to the splendid sight of Baynards Station in all its original finery. South-east of Baynards the route crosses the River Arun by a curious two-tiered bridge, then heads towards the southern outskirts of Horsham. Here the path leaves the railway track for a short diversion along quiet country lanes to Christ's Hospital School where the southern railway link is joined.

Between Southwater and Partridge Green the way makes a determined curve towards the south and crosses a series of fields well away from the village and only rarely coming close to individual houses or farms. Then towards Henfield the Downs begin to rise ahead as an enticing wall on the horizon. The countryside opens out, views become wider, there are crossings of the River Adur to be made, with a number of attractive alternative paths beckoning along the river's banks, or traversing the lowlands that moat the South Downs.

After Henfield you swing south-westwards and take to a farm road winding down to historic Bramber, whose solitary finger of flint wall gives barely a hint of the important Norman castle fortress that once stood on a mound now surrounded by trees. One last short stretch through the flat meadows of the Adur's valley leads to the hamlet of Botolphs and the crossing of the South Downs Way.

★ ★ ★

THE DOWNS LINK - SOUTH BOUND
(ST. MARTHA'S TO BOTOLPHS)

SECTION 1:   ST. MARTHA'S HILL TO CRANLEIGH

Distance:	9 miles
Maps:	O.S. Landranger series; Sheets 186 *Aldershot, Guildford & Surrounding Area* and 187 *Dorking, Reigate & Crawley Area* 1:50,000
Accommodation:	Guildford - Guest-house, b&b

St. Martha's Hill stands two miles east of Guildford. It rises north of the village of Chilworth, and to the west of the neat little community of Albury. A prominent wooded vantage point topped by a 19th century church bearing parts that date from the 11th century, it enjoys magnificent views over the Weald of Surrey and along the Greensand Ridge which spreads away to the east in a projection of tree-crowned hills. There are car parks to the east and the west of St. Martha's, each one about a third of a mile from the summit, thus encouraging many visitors to its slopes in the summer for gentle walks and picnics. The North Downs Way crosses the summit along a well-trodden sandy path dodging in and out of the trees.

Access by road is easiest via a narrow lane that crosses the ridge between Chilworth (A248) and the A25 in Guildford. By rail Chilworth station (1 mile south of St. Martha's) lies on the Guildford to Dorking line.

★ ★ ★

From St. Martha's church (1) (Grid ref: 027483) head east on the sandy footpath of the North Downs Way for about 400 yards, steadily

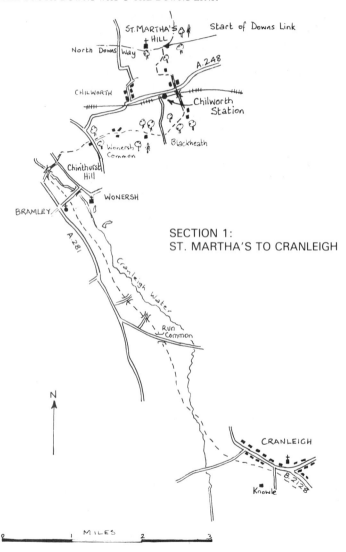

SECTION 1:
ST. MARTHA'S TO CRANLEIGH

descending among trees. Shortly before coming to a war-time pillbox the start of the Downs Link is marked by a wooden fingerpost on the right, and a stone marker bearing the Downs Link symbol dated 1984. From these two markers a clear sandy path heads down through the trees (lush with bluebells in spring) with views into the green Tilling-bourne Valley below. The path soon becomes a sunken track among oaks, then along the left-hand side of a field to meet a crossing track. Turn left and follow this as it crosses the Tilling Bourne stream, passes Lockner Farm and comes to the A248 road on the outskirts of Chilworth village.

Cross the road and continue straight ahead on a track leading between cottages. It goes over a railway bridge and shortly after you wander along a sandy path running parallel with a long driveway. The path leads between hedges and trees - soon becomes almost a tunnel of trees - and on the edge of woodland passes a cluster of houses and comes to a crossing track, or driveway. Straight ahead the path divides. Go half-right into the mixed woods of Blackheath.

Maintain direction through the woods and you will come onto Sample Oak Lane with the Blackheath sign nearby on the left. Cross the lane and continue straight ahead on a broad track going over a large heath of gorse, birch and broom; pass a solitary house on the left and continue ahead alongside a fence. There are stands of Scots pine all around, squirrels chasing along the branches, jays squawking, song birds trilling; a very pleasant stretch of wood and heath. The track narrows and begins to descend, now a sandy, deeply sunken trail with badger setts in the banks. The path is then contained by hedges and, passing a farm, you come onto a farm road and walk past Great Tangley Manor. About 50 yards before reaching the B2128 road bear right along a bridleway to cross a corner of Wonersh Common, coming to the road soon after, opposite Forge Cottage. (Grid ref: 016463)

Cross the road and take the continuing path which leads down the right-hand side of the cottage. The tree-lined way forks after 200 yards or so and you take the right branch to pass along the lower northern slopes of Chinthurst Hill. Soon along the path there are fine views to the right looking across the Tillingbourne Valley to St. Martha's Hill. The track then swings left, on being joined by another path, and deteriorates to a muddy sunken way among trees and hedges, then brings you to Old Chinthurst Farm and a minor road.

Go over the road and walk straight ahead along another minor road that very soon brings you to a pair of bridges; the smaller of the two crossing the overgrown Wey and Arun Canal (2), and the larger bridge built to take the road across the former railway line. Cross the smaller bridge and immediately turn left to follow the clear track along the course of the Guildford-Horsham railway. (On the right the river - Cranleigh Water, a tributary of the Wey - comes rushing over a weir by some houses, and is a most attractive feature.)

As a bridge built here to carry the railway over the river has been demolished, the track veers left, then among trees to resume the original line ahead, now having lost the river's company. For a short stretch there are houses nearby, then you walk through what was formerly Bramley and Wonersh Station, its platform sign remaining to this day. (The obvious station buildings have been taken over by a builders' merchant.) Bridle gates take you over the road which links the villages of Bramley and Wonersh, and you then continue ahead. (Refreshments at a pub in Wonersh to the left.)

Along a section of embankment you can look down onto gardens, some of which have made the most of the stream that flows through them. Now the route runs parallel with the A281 Guildford to Horsham road. On the left the rather sluggish green stream of Cranleigh Water that rejoins the route is a sad reminder of the one-time busy Wey and Arun Canal. For a while now the Downs Link is shared by the Wey-South Path. (3)

Soon heading through countryside with the main road veering away, the route takes you through flowery banks, under two bridges and on to a third leading beneath a road at Run Common. After passing a woodland the winding Cranleigh Water stream is seen making ox-bows through the fields on the left. The route curves slightly and comes along the southern edge of the substantial village of Cranleigh - said to be England's largest. (4) (Shops and refreshments.)

Things Seen On The Way:

1: *St. Martha's Church* is the parish church of Chilworth, down in the valley. It is open on Sundays and Bank Holidays throughout the year, and on other days at specified times. (There is a notice giving these times outside the church.) Services are held there every Sunday, despite its remoteness. There has been a church on this hilltop site since the 11th century, and it is thought probable that the prominent site was earlier used for the celebration of a form of heathen worship. From the church there are extensive and delightful views.

2: *Wey and Arun Canal.* This canal, completed in 1816 to link the Thames with the River Arun and thus with the South Coast, was originally designed for military purposes, but after the Napoleonic Wars it had a commercial use until the coming of the railway made it financially impractical. In 1868 the canal closed, but in recent years a Trust has been set up with the aim of restoring it for navigation once more.

3: *The Wey-South Path* follows the towpath of the former Wey and Arun canal where possible, and in places coincides with the Downs Link. This 36-mile walk begins at the town bridge in Guildford, and finishes in Amberley at the foot of the South Downs. (See Section 8 of the South Downs Way route.) A guide to the Wey-South Path, written by Aeneas Mackintosh, is available from: The Secretary, The Wey and Arun Canal Trust Ltd., 24 Griffiths Ave., Lancing, West Sussex, BN15 0HW.

4: *Cranleigh* claims still to be the largest village in England, although many would see it today as a town. Cranleigh School (founded 1865) is well known, its chapel a handsome building while the parish church has a fine 14th century tower. The Village Hospital dates from 1859 and is said to be the first of its kind in the country. On the outskirts of the village a Roman brickworks was discovered.

Accommodation:

Guildford	B.&J. Newman's Guest-house, 24 Waterden Road, Guildford, GU1 2AY. Tel: Guildford 60558
	Mr. Parsons, Greyfriars, 9 Castle Hill, Guildford, GU1 3SX. Tel: Guildford 61795
	Mrs. Atkinson, 129 Stoke Road, Guildford, GU1 1ET. Tel: Guildford 38260

SECTION 2:   **CRANLEIGH TO RUDGWICK**

Distance:	4 miles
Map:	O.S. Landranger series; Sheet 187 *Dorking, Reigate & Crawley Area* 1:50,000
Accommodation:	Rudgwick - Hotel

This very short section takes the route along the western outskirts of Cranleigh and into a quiet stretch of countryside; mostly large meadows and woodlands. Baynards Station is reached on the boundary of Baynards Park Estate. (The gates leading to the big Tudor house of Baynards Park are seen a few paces beyond the station.) Then into flower-rich woodlands on a path that has temporarily lost the railway, for the line used to go

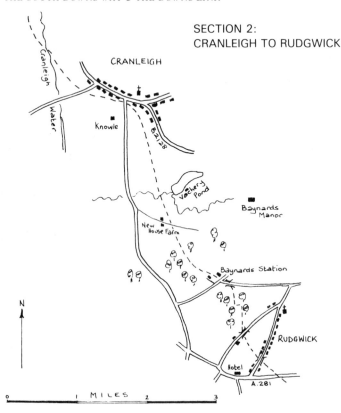

through a tunnel here, but on closure of the line the tunnel was filled in. The village of Rudgwick lies beyond the woods, and there's an hotel a short distance away alongside the A281, for those in need of accommodation.

On this stage the Downs Link leaves Surrey and crosses into West Sussex.

★ ★ ★

The route is clear as it skirts Cranleigh village. On crossing round the edge of a car park you may see a large house a few fields away, standing among trees. This is Knowle. You wander between sports fields

120

Baynards Station

and then resume the journey along the former railway track, hemmed in by hedges and trees for a while, and among them you will see a railway signal remaining on the right. The last few houses of Cranleigh are passed and it's back to fields and meadows once more.

With open countryside all around the track goes through a cutting lined with trees whose branches meet overhead. An embankment follows on emerging from the cutting, and unseen off to the left is Vachery Pond, thought to be a hammer pond from the days of the important Wealden iron industry. (A footpath, with steps down from the main track, leads to it and on to Baynards Park, for those who have time to make an interesting diversion.)

At the entrance to New House Farm a pretty rhododendron-banked pond is seen on the right. Soon after you go among woods that are bright with bluebells in spring, the embankment yellow with primroses and wild clematis scrambling among some of the trees.

After passing at the bottom of a few gardens you come to the Thurlow Arms pub and Baynards Station, now a private residence, but still in its former railway finery. (The platforms appear ready to receive a steam train; on station doors there are still signs for Porters and Lamp Room. The whole scene is extremely pleasing on the eye, and it is good to see a notice proclaiming that the building received an

121

award from the Surrey Industrial History Group in 1985.) Please respect the privacy of those who live here and be discreet in your interest and enthusiasm for this former station.

Turn left along the side of the station, then right at the gates of Baynards Park Estate once again on the track of the former railway, and a short distance ahead you will come to a road bridge. The cutting ahead formerly entered a tunnel, now filled in. Here the bridleway and footpath routes diverge.

Walkers' Route: Continue along the track, and at the end of a short open section go up some steps onto the top of what was Baynards Tunnel, and into a patch of woodland. At a junction of tracks bear right on a path which runs along the left-hand edge of the glorious wood anemone and bluebell bright South Wood (crossing from Surrey into West Sussex). Cross a stile and bear left, following a footpath down through the woods and join the main track at a crossing path. This is the Sussex Border Path. (1)

Bridleway: After passing beneath the road bridge turn left to go onto the road, then left again over the bridge. Soon after you will see the continuing bridleway signposted on the left leading through the woods. The way leads between banks of rhododendrons, then swings left and goes down a slope to a junction of tracks. Turn right here and about 100 yards further on you rejoin the main track.

Heading south the Downs Link track goes beneath a brick-built road bridge and, under a second bridge, passes through Rudgwick.

Rudgwick has a brick works, one or two attractive buildings, perhaps the best being The Queen's Head pub to the north of the village, and an hotel to the south. To reach the hotel go up onto the road and walk south along it for about 400 yards to reach the A281. Turn right and the hotel lies a few yards away.

Things Seen On The Way:
1: *The Sussex Border Path*, as its name suggests, attempts to follow the county boundary from Emsworth to Rye. Total distance is about 150 miles. Route guide: *The Sussex Border Path* by Ben Perkins and Aeneas Mackintosh. (From: Ben Perkins, 11 Old London Road, Brighton, BN1 8XR.)

SECTION 3:   **RUDGWICK TO CHRIST'S HOSPITAL**

Distance: 5 miles
Map: O.S. Landranger series; Sheet 187   *Dorking,*
                    Reigate & Crawley Area   1:50,000
Accommodation: None on route

This stage of the walk resumes across open countryside heading south-
eastwards. Early on the way goes over the River Arun by a curious double-
decked bridge, and towards Slinfold leads through part of Park Street
Nature Reserve. A little to the west of Slinfold the Downs Link is crossed
by the A29. The road had its origins in Roman times, for this was part of
Stane Street, the great Roman highway leading from Chichester to London.
(See also details on Section 8 of the South Downs Way route.) That Roman
past is recalled alongside this road; there's Roman Station, (or Roman
Gate) and Roman Woods. And legend has it that a bell, on its way from
Rome to York during the occupation of Britain, fell into marshy ground
near Slinfold and was lost.

East of Slinfold there's more open countryside, and having passed
beneath the A264 south of Broadbridge Heath, it is not long before the
original railway track is deserted for a while and a series of country lanes
lead to the 'bluecoat school' of Christ's Hospital.

* * *

Cross the busy A281 Guildford to Horsham road on the edge of
Rudgley. (Grid ref: 090330) Half-right ahead the way resumes
through a bridle gate and up a slope to an embankment. Very soon
along this embankment you cross the River Arun by a two-tiered
bridge, built so at the insistence of the Railways Inspector in order to
reduce the gradient of the line to Rudgwick Station.

A drizzle had begun to fall, and as I was growing hungry I clambered
down the bank and sat beneath the bridge on the side of the river to eat my
sandwiches. It was dry down there; dry and protected from the cool wind.
Wild garlic grew in clumps nearby, the white starred flowers appearing far
lovelier than their fragrance would indicate. It was peaceful on the banks of
the Arun whose water was muddy and sluggish, but there were birds singing
happily all around unconcerned by the rain, and their songs served to remind
me that once this bridge would have thundered with the passage of trains.
Great clouds of smoke would have puffed over the trees, and the fragrance
of wild garlic would no doubt have been mingled with the smell of coal

123

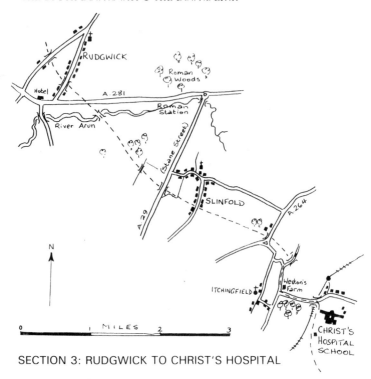

SECTION 3: RUDGWICK TO CHRIST'S HOSPITAL

smoke and oil. The romance of the age of steam was lost on me then, and I was selfishly well content to have the track to myself as a pleasant walking route; alone with the birds and the rabbits and the smell of wild garlic untarnished by coal smoke. By the time I'd finished my lunch the rain had stopped and a weak sun braved the clouds. That sun was greeted by the birds with the same enthusiasm with which they'd welcomed the rain.

Beyond the bridge there's a conifer plantation on the left, and a few old crab apple trees alongside the track. Towards Slinfold, as you wander through Park Street Nature Reserve, you'll pass a number of marker posts of a nature trail. A brick arched bridge takes a track over the Downs Link route, and soon after you go through a cutting and come to another bridge with Stane Street (A29) passing overhead. There's a factory on the right as you continue ahead along a motorable track, and when the track bears left in front of a house, you turn with it, and immediately on your right you will see two lesser tracks running parallel with each other. Take the left-hand of these which is the continuing Downs Link. It brings you to a row of houses in a residential street in well-kept Slinfold. (Grid ref: 117308) Cross the street and maintain direction, and within a few yards you are once more travelling through open country with meadows on either side and woodlands crowning the low distant hills.

The hedge-lined track brings you to the traffic thunder of the A264 south of Broadbridge Heath. Happily the route passes beneath the road, and soon after you gaze directly ahead at a tower rising above meadows and trees: this is at Christ's Hospital School. A little under half a mile beyond the A264 you approach another bridge and the way deserts the route of the railway line, swings left for about 30 yards to reach a country lane (Mill Lane), and there turns right. Cross the bridge and follow Mill Lane as it winds between fields and brings you to a road junction where you bear left. About 150 yards beyond Weston's Farm turn left on the country road leading to Christ's Hospital School (1) (Opposite this turning there is a footpath which leads across the fields to the lovely church of St. Nicholas at Itchingfield.)

For perhaps the first time since leaving St. Martha's you now have a real impression of space. Gazing off to the left as you wander along Christ's Hospital Road, you see way across the complex meadows, fields and woodlands of the Weald to the blue line of the Greensand Ridge, with Holmbury Hill and Leith Hill as the major points along it.

Cross a railway bridge and take the right fork beyond it. The buildings of Christ's Hospital School make a formidable impression across the trim lawns. Immediately before the white school gates, bear right through a fence onto a footpath to pass in front of a cottage. Go beyond a clump of horse chestnut trees and along a clear path running alongside a railway line. To the left stretch the school playing fields.

Things Seen On The Way:
1: *Christ's Hospital School.* Founded by Edward VI the original school was destroyed by the Great Fire of London. It was moved to its present site in 1902; a rambling mixture of architectural styles in extensive grounds.

SECTION 4:   **CHRIST'S HOSPITAL TO**
                 PARTRIDGE GREEN

Distance: 7 miles
Map: O.S. Landranger series; Sheet 198 *Brighton &*
                 The Downs 1:50,000
Accommodation: None on route

About 1½ miles from Christ's Hospital the route diverts slightly from the bed of the railway and takes you through Southwater, where there will be an opportunity to buy snacks and drinks from a village store. Southwater once had a thriving brick making industry, although this has now gone, while an area of flooded clay pits that once formed part of this industry remains on the south side of the route and has been adopted as a country park.

After passing beneath the busy dual carriageway of the A24 the way leads into a broad landscape of meadowlands and spinneys. All that remains of West Grinstead Station are the former platforms, now overgrown and some distance from the hamlet after which the station was named. Then more farmland with the South Downs growing in the distance as you approach the village of Partridge Green.

There will be several opportunities for refreshment on this stage of the walk.

* * *

As you walk along the path beside the railway, with the playing fields of Christ's Hospital School spreading on your left, you approach a row of cottages. Just before reaching them bear half-right along a stony path enclosed by hedges, and continue in the same direction once more following the bed of the old railway line. (The modern railway has veered away to the right now.) A short distance along this track you gain the first views of the South Downs in the distance half-right ahead.

The way leads through a series of white field gates near Watlings Farm, then under a bridge carrying a minor road at Two Mile Ash. (Grid ref: 147272) Emerging on the eastern side of the bridge you will see a pub, The Castle, above to the left.

Half a mile later, on the outskirts of Southwater, you come to a concrete farm drive near a barn. Turn right and wander along this away from the line of the old railway track, heading towards a church.

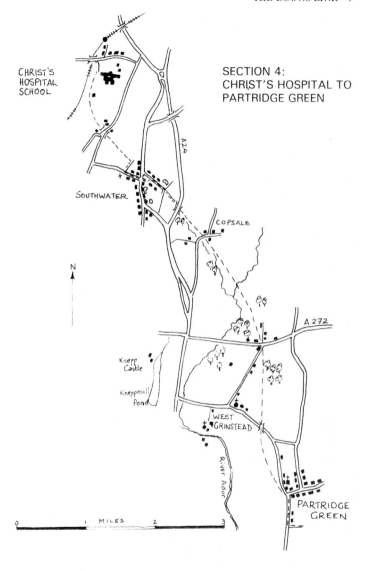

CHRIST'S
HOSPITAL
SCHOOL

SECTION 4:
CHRIST'S HOSPITAL TO
PARTRIDGE GREEN

A24

SOUTHWATER

COPSALE

N

A 272

Knepp
Castle

Kneppmill
Pond

WEST
GRINSTEAD

River Adur

PARTRIDGE
GREEN

0   1   MILES   2   3

You come onto a road opposite a cemetery and turn left to walk into Southwater village. On reaching a little crossroads by The Cock Inn (food store nearby) cross straight ahead into Andrews Lane. About 30 yards later turn left just before the telephone exchange. Follow the exchange boundary fence, then turn right along the obvious bed of the old railway.

On the outer edge of Southwater you pass the flooded clay pits off to your right, descend half-left down some steps into a car parking area, and cross Cripplegate Lane into Stakers Lane which you follow south-eastwards and near the end wander beneath the Southwater by-pass (A24). Maintain direction, go up a slope onto an embankment and continue ahead along the obvious Downs Link route, soon passing woods that are massed with huge drifts of wild garlic (ramsons) in springtime. Off to your left you can see Copsale Court, and soon after the track brings you down to a narrow lane at the hamlet of Copsale by The Bridge House pub. (Grid ref: 171249)

Between Copsale and the A272 lies a two-mile stretch through a continuing landscape of gentle, open fields and pastures lined with hedgerows, dotted with spinneys and woodland shaws. Trackside woods are rich with flowers, as is the track itself. (Bugle and primroses making a bright pattern of blue on gold along one particular length of embankment.) The route crosses one of the tributaries of the River Adur which it will follow now, sometimes as a close companion, sometimes separated by a field or two, all the way to Botolphs. As you approach the road bridge carrying the A272 so you pass the overgrown platforms of the former West Grinstead Station. (To the right, a short step along the A272, refreshments are available at a Little Chef café.)

For the next two miles or so the way heads almost due south and, with the countryside opening, the South Downs show themselves more clearly, with Chanctonbury Ring standing out on the skyline to the south-east as an obvious mound to direct men's attention. Wandering through a low cutting here in late April/May you may be greeted by the colourful spikes of early purple orchids. It is a very pleasant part of the walk, springy underfoot, studded with flowers and with growing views ahead.

A little to the east of West Grinstead the route crosses the B2135 on a bridge, and soon after this you may notice in a farmyard off to the left, a railway signal standing forlorn and without purpose. Later there are one or two crossing paths, but the main track continues on course for Partridge Green. The tower of the village church can shortly be seen among houses to the left of the track, and then the track goes up to meet a road on the southern edge of the village. (Grid ref: 189190)

Partridge Green grew around the railway during the last century, but with its demise the village has expanded and today there's a trading estate on the site of the former station. Partridge Green has a pub (The Partridge), shop and Post Office.

SECTION 5:   **PARTRIDGE GREEN TO BOTOLPHS**

Distance:	8 miles
Map:	O.S. Landranger series; Sheet 198 *Brighton &*
	The Downs 1:50,000
Accommodation:	Bramber - Hotel
	Steyning - Hotel, Guest-house, b&b
	Truleigh Hill - Youth Hostel (off route, 2 miles
	from end)

This final section of the route experiences the most open countryside of the whole Downs Link as it works a way over low-lying pastures cut by watercourses at the foot of the Downs. The Downs themselves grow steadily more impressive as a substantial wall of green barring all hint of the nearby sea. The River Adur is a major feature of this stage, and it is tempting in places to desert the track of the old railway in favour of one of the riverbank walks. (Those who fall for this temptation can avoid the brief visit to Henfield, though they'll not save any mileage.) It is also possible to follow the Adur all the way from the pastures south of Partridge Green to the South Downs Way bridge at Botolphs, thus losing the railway route but having the river for company for the final 6½ miles of the walk.

On the edge of Bramber (east of Steyning) it is worth making a very short diversion to look at the singular remains of Bramber Castle. Then it's a last meadowland stroll to the tiny scattered hamlet of Botolphs and the end of the Downs Link.

*   *   *

On reaching the B2135 road at Partridge Green turn right and follow it south for about 400 yards, passing the lovely crooked-beamed Yew Tree Cottage, then head to the left along a farm road which goes to Homelands Farm. The road deteriorates to a rough track and curves a little to the left. On reaching cross-tracks turn right to rejoin the original route. At the end of this hedged section go through a bridle gate into a large open pasture with Henfield seen directly ahead, about

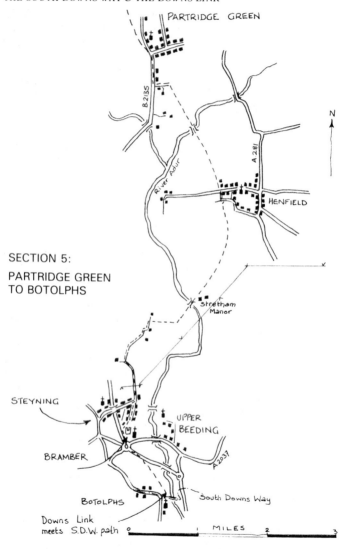

PARTRIDGE GREEN

B.2135

N

River Adur

A 281

HENFIELD

SECTION 5:

PARTRIDGE GREEN
TO BOTOLPHS

Stretham
Manor

STEYNING

UPPER
BEEDING

BRAMBER

A 2037

BOTOLPHS

South Downs Way

Downs Link
meets S.D.W. path

0   1   MILES   2   3

a mile and a half away. Beyond that the masts on top of Truleigh Hill are clearly visible. Walk ahead along a grassy path to cross the River Adur and continue beyond it on an obvious track leading though a cutting to Henfield.

Note: Those wishing to follow the river to the end of the walk should go down to the left bank at this first crossing, and keep with it heading downstream to the next point where the Downs Link crosses by Stretham Manor. Then go over to the right bank and follow this to Botolphs.

The Downs Link route arrives in Henfield by the Cat and Canary pub. Bear left along the road and then take the first turning on the right (shops on the left). At the bottom of the road bear right and, a few yards later, go left on an enclosed track. On coming to crossing tracks by some houses continue straight ahead, through a bridle gate and beside sturdy fences. For a while hedges restrict the views, but now and again you catch a glimpse of the enlarging Downs and know that the end of the walk is approaching.

The route crosses one or two minor water-courses and comes to Stretham Manor, an old timbered building on the left of the track, and crosses the Adur again. (It was near here that the Romans had a crossing in the first century AD. A footpath nearby heads east along the course of the old Roman road and comes to Woods Mill, headquarters of the Sussex Trust for Nature Conservation.)

About half a mile after having crossed the river, leave the main track and bear right up the bank to go through a bridle gate, over a stile and along the edge of a field heading west. You come to a rough farm road and turn left along it to walk down towards Wyckham Farm. (Grid ref: 190131) Continue past the farm along the road as it winds among fields and pastures, passing barns and a sewage treatment works, and at last you will come to the village of Bramber. (1)

The road swings right after Kings Barn Farm, and you then bear left into Kingstone Avenue. (Kings Barn Lane continues ahead to Steyning. (2)) At the end of Kingstone Avenue turn left and walk straight ahead, ignoring the road which bears round to the right, and you will arrive at a roundabout on the A283. (Bramber Castle stands up a sloping drive to the left; the Norman church is next to it.)

Cross the roundabout to the A283 Shoreham road and follow the right-hand verge for about 400 yards. You then go through a gateway on the right to rejoin the railway bed, which is little more than a grassy track here. You soon come to a clear stony track which takes you to the end of the Downs Link, with the River Adur to the left.

The track comes to an abrupt end where the South Downs Way

crosses. There is a Downs Link information board beside this crossing. The hamlet of Botolphs (3) lies to the right, through a gap, and the church of St. Botolph's is a short stroll away to the south.

Things Seen On The Way:

1: *Bramber* has become virtually joined to its neighbouring village of Steyning, wedged between the river and the Downs. The castle remains are of a Norman structure of 1083, built by William de Braose, whose family came to live here. Originally more than 50 yards long, the grey flint-walled fortress was built on a bend in the river to defend the gap in the Downs created by the Adur, but the castle was beseiged during the Civil War by the Roundheads and all that stands today is a single finger of keep wall and the mound of earthworks. Bramber Castle is in the care of the National Trust. Nearby stands a rather stumpy Norman church, also built shortly after the Conquest by William de Braose.

2: *Steyning* has some lovely well-preserved buildings; there are 16th and 17th century houses in Church Street and Georgian buildings in the High Street. The parish church of St. Andrew's is Norman on a Saxon site. In the porch lies the slab of a tomb said to belong to the father of King Alfred, Aethelwulf of Wessex. Steyning was a port until the Adur silted up during the 14th century.

3: *Botolphs* is but a shadow of the former community that once lived here. For until the Middle Ages the village prospered by fishing and through its own salt industry. Then the sea withdrew from the valley of the Adur and altered the future of this little place. Today there are but a few cottages, a farm or two, and the Saxon church dedicated to the English missionary, St. Botolph.

Accommodation:

Bramber	Green Leaves Hotel, Clays Hill, Bramber, Steyning, BN4 3WE. Tel: Steyning 813222
Steyning	Steyning House Hotel, High Street, Steyning, BN4 3RD. Tel: Steyning 812041
	Mrs. Barnicott, Down House Guest-House, King's Barn Villas, Steyning, BN4 3FA. Tel: Steyning 812319
	Mr. Morrow, 5 Coxham Lane, Steyning, BN4 3LG. Tel: Steyning 812286

Truleigh Hill   The Youth Hostel, Tottington Barn, Truleigh Hill,
                  Shoreham-by-Sea, BN4 5FB. Tel: Steyning 813419

Public Transport:
Buses run from Upper Beeding to Shoreham-by-Sea, and from there
to Brighton for trains to London.

The singular remains of Bramber Castle

USEFUL ADDRESSES

The Ramblers' Association
1-5 Wandsworth Road
London SW8 2LJ

Southern Tourist Board
Town Hall Centre
Eastleigh
Hants SO5 4DE

The Society of Sussex Downsmen
93 Church Road
Hove
East Sussex BN3 2BA

Youth Hostels Association
Trevelyan House
St. Albans
Herts AL1 2DY

South-East England Tourist Board
1 Warwick Park
Tunbridge Wells
Kent TN2 5BR

East Sussex County Council
Southover House
Lewes
East Sussex BN7 1YA

West Sussex County Council
County Hall
Chichester
West Sussex PO19 1RQ

Surrey County Council
County Hall
Kingston-upon-Thames
Surrey GU7 1HR

Waverley Borough Council
The Burys
Godalming
Surrey KT1 2DN

*Alfriston High Street, looking towards the
Old Market Cross*

RECOMMENDED FURTHER READING

The following list will give a background of information on the countryside through which these two walks lead. It is, of course, a small selection only and browsing through your public library will no doubt expand the coverage further.

Baker, M.	*Sussex Villages* (Robert Hale)
Brandon, P.	*The Sussex Landscape* (Hodder & Stoughton)
Darby, B.	*View of Sussex* (Robert Hale)
Harrison, D.	*Along the South Downs* (Cassell)
Hillier, C. & Mosley, J.	*Images of the Downs* (McMillan)
Jebb, M.	*A Guide to the South Downs Way* (Constable)
Mason, O.	*South-East England* (Bartholomew)
Mee, A.	*The King's England - Hampshire* (Hodder & Stoughton)
	The King's England - Surrey
	The King's England - Sussex
O'Dell, N.	*Portrait of Hampshire* (Robert Hale)
Scholes, R.	*Understanding the Countryside* (Moorland Publishing Co)
Spence, K.	*The Companion Guide to Kent & Sussex* (Collins)
White, J.T.	*The South-East, Down and Weald* (Eyre-Methuen)
Woodford, C.	*Portrait of Sussex* (Robert Hale)

Printed by Carnmor Print & Design,
95/97, London Road, Preston, Lancashire.